Heroines
THREE PLAYS

John Murrell
Sharon Pollock
Michel Tremblay

Edited by Joyce Doolittle

Red Deer College Press

The Publishers
Red Deer College Press
56 Avenue & 32 Street Box 5005
Red Deer Alberta Canada T4N 5H5

Acknowledgments
The Publishers gratefully acknowledge the financial contribution of
The Alberta Foundation for the Arts, Alberta Culture & Multiculturalism,
The Canada Council and Red Deer College.

Credits
Edited for the Press by Joyce Doolittle.
Designed by Dennis Johnson.
Printed and bound in Canada by Best Gagné
Printing Ltée for Red Deer College Press.
Special thanks to Patricia Roy for her assistance
in the preparation of this book.

On the Cover: Pat Galloway (top) as Sarah Bernhardt in the Stratford Festival production of *Memoir;* photo by David Cooper, courtesy of the Stratford Festival. Susan Wright (centre) as Eme in Factory Theatre Studio Café production of *Getting it Straight;* photo by Nir Bareket, courtesy of the Factory Theatre Studio Café. Richard Monette (bottom) as Hosanna in the Tarragon Theatre production of *Hosanna;* photo courtesy of the Tarragon Theatre Archives, Archival Collections, University of Guelph.

Canadian Cataloguing in Publication Data

Contents: Hosanna / Michel Tremblay — Getting it straight /
Sharon Pollock — Memoir / John Murrell.
ISBN 0-88995-081-4
1. Canadian drama (English)–20th Century.
I. Tremblay, Michel, 1942– Hosanna   II. Pollock, Sharon, 1936– Getting it
Straight III.   Murrell, John, 1945– Memoir   IV. Doolittle, Joyce, 1928–

PS8307.H47 1992 C812'.5408 C91-091846-5
PR9196.3.H47 1992

Library of Congress Cataloging in Publication Data

Pollock, Sharon.
Heroines / by Sharon Pollock, John Murrell, Michel Tremblay;
introduction by Joyce Doolittle.
p. cm.
ISBN 0-88734-624-3 $10.95
1. Canadian drama—20th century.   2. Bernhardt, Sarah, 1844 – 1923
—Drama.   3. Women—Drama.   I. Murrell, John. II. Tremblay,
Michel, 1942 – .   III. Title.
PR9196.6.P58   1992
812'.54080352042—dc20   92 – 54101
CIP

CONTENTS

COUNTERPARTS
An Introduction

Carl Jung's theory that human beings have both male and female characteristics is so familiar to us that it seems self-evident. Nonetheless, masculine and feminine roles are more ambiguous and troublesome today than ever before. Despite this, my intuitive choice of *Heroines* for the title of this collection must have sprung from Jung's theory. Each of the principal characters in *Heroines* has complicated mixtures of so-called masculine and feminine attributes. The two women, Sarah Bernhardt of John Murrell's *Memoir* and Eme of Sharon Pollock's *Getting it Straight,* often have more stereotypical male characteristics than female, and Claude, of Michel Tremblay's *Hosanna,* emulates the arch-romantic woman within the man. In turn, the males in *Memoir* and *Hosanna* have qualities often considered feminine. Bernhardt's secretary, Pitou, is modest and self-effacing, and Cuirette is ultimately tender towards Hosanna. In *Getting it Straight,* we meet all secondary characters, male and female, through Eme's eyes only. Her husband is one dimensional, a symbol to her of male misuse of power. The lack of an active, masculine "other" may be one reason that Eme is mad.

The lead character in each of these plays is at a crossroad. Sarah Bernhardt faces death. Eme fights madness. Claude painfully searches for himself. And at these crossroads, time is suspended to allow each a desperate re-view and re-creation of his or her atypical role(s) in "normal" society. Sarah and Eme play many parts; Hosanna is consumed by one. The setting of each play is widely variant, but the tools the characters use to deal with pain and transcend reality are similar. They relive the past, they role play, they face their demons, and with varying degrees of success and grace, they accept themselves.

For Sarah, acting out is professional. It is reality that is a fantasy. She spends her last days by the sea in Brittany, ostensibly writing her second book of memoirs. The edge of the ocean holds the prospect that she can be in touch with both psyche and ego, and be able to pass between the two. Sarah does this by using her craft to confront painful memories and by enlisting the aid of faithful Pitou, who reluctantly plays "the other" to her various former selves. Images of nature permeate the play, particularly that of the sun, with which the heroine identifies. The drama unfolds in a grand space, a romantic nineteenth century milieu, a theatre suitable to the icon of an era.

At the end of the play, Sarah prepares for death in the best way she knows, through a rehearsal. A young playwright has sent her his script. It is set in fifteenth century Spain, and the heroine is a young Moorish girl. As she reads the peasant girl's entrance speech, Bernhardt, we realize, is making her final exit.

> *[...SARAH stands slowly, carefully, then moves forward without the least difficulty, very graceful, very young. She is a Moorish girl, wading into the margin of the Guadalquivir. Suddenly she stops and looks up into the brightening morning light.]*

SARAH: *[To the sun or to herself, trembling; an even younger voice]*
"They say in Heaven there is an herb, which heals all wounds, even those of love. But are the people of my dark race permitted to wander the roads of Heaven? I am so afraid!"

> *[Pause. Music. SARAH takes a step or two back and drops the character of the Moorish girl. Still very young, as herself, she smiles luminously up into the sunlight.]*

fin

Eme, in *Getting it Straight,* brims over with guilt and responsibility, and becomes consumed by her schizophrenia, a condition that encourages improvisation and includes offstage voices. She has escaped her keepers and is hiding under the bleachers of a rodeo, using the departed public's debris as props in the pretend games that make up her reality. The grand stand she then takes against the obscenity of male aggression, particularly the atomic bomb, is grotesquely mirrored by her grandstand hideout. She sees the sky only through the slats of the empty audience bleachers, as something she is cut off from. Night falls, lights go on, and celestial bodies group and regroup—in her mind. Despite the schizophrenic confusion of reality and fantasy, the hostile sky from which the

real bomb was dropped ("white rain garnet red the clouds")
becomes, in the play's final lines, poetic and powerful—but it
remains ambiguous, as does Eme's fate and our own.

you
and I
spin a gossamer net of women's hands and rapunzel's
hair and that net will encircle the globe and if a
person stood on the far left star of the utmost
edge of cassiopeia's chair that net would twinkle
in the inky cosmos like fairy lights on a christmas
tree—and what would it spell?

what would it spell?

what would it spell?

> *fin*

The only stars in *Hosanna* are manmade in Hollywood. Nature is
masked by decadent civilization. The night sky flashes neon outside the window of Hosanna's bachelor apartment, and new garish
lights in Parc La Fontaine make buying momentary sexual plea-
sures impossible. Cuirette, Hosanna's live-in lover, resents both
forms of illumination vehemently.

Their apartment is an unremarkable, cramped, urban space. The
most visible objects are a mirror, a bed, a bad original painting and
an even worse reproduction of a sculpture. Amidst the squalor,
beauty becomes a primary concern. "Mirror, mirror on the wall.
Who's the fairest of them all?" is the question Hosanna asks herself
over and over again. But, like Snow White's stepmother, Hosanna,
the (drag) Queen must face her inevitable aging. The business of
beauty is her day-to-day job as a hairdresser, and through it she has
come to equate glitter with glamour and glamour with love. Over
the years, Hosanna has learned to hide her loneliness behind layers
of lies: behind her garish mask of pop persona Elizabeth Taylor por-
traying an archetypal queen, Cleopatra, and behind her quintessen-
tial tinseltown version of Cleopatra's history. For Hosanna to admit
her sex, her love, and her masculinity, she must have the courage

to be "alone with Claude." In the last scene of the play, she does this and becomes, of all three heroines in this collection, the most honest and the most transformed.

HOSANNA: Cleopatra is dead, and the Parc La Fontaine is all lit up!

> *[She gets up, takes off her underpants and turns slowly towards CUIRETTE.]*

Look, Raymond, I'm a man.... I'm a man, Raymond.... I'm a man. I'm a man.... I'm a man.

> *[RAYMOND gets up, goes toward CLAUDE, and takes him in his arms.]*

> *Slow fade.]*

> *fin*

Three remarkable characters. Each tries to get it straight and each asks: *Who am I? What is my role in the universe? What is my responsibility?* Each attempts a memoir, embellishes and unmasks potent private myths, clings to or destroys precious talismans, and faces final moments with courage, intelligence, and creativity. Hosannas are appropriate for them all.

Joyce Doolittle
Calgary, Alberta
March, 1992

Memoir

"Je mourrai en scène. C'est mon champ de bataille."
—Sarah Bernhardt

JOHN MURRELL

Pat Galloway [Sarah Bernhardt] and Douglas Chamberlain [Georges Pitou] in the Stratford Festival production, Stratford, Ontario, 1990. Directed by Albert Millaire. Set design by Christina Poddubiuk. Lighting by Kevin Fraser. Photo by David Cooper, courtesy of the Stratford Festival.

Characters in the Play
SARAH BERNHARDT, an actress
GEORGES PITOU, her secretary

Author's Note
In this play I have departed from historical fact in one significant manner: I have kept Pitou in Madame Bernhardt's service longer than she did herself. It is doubtful whether he was still with her during her final summer, although he did for many years scribble and organize notes for a second volume of her memoirs, which she never completed.

All translations in this text from other authors are my own.

There may be one interval at the conclusion of the first part. A successful French production of the piece and another at the Stratford Festival of Canada were played without interval and lasted between ninety and one hundred minutes.

> [*The single setting for the play is a terrace, vaguely attached to a large rambling manor house, which may be glimpsed in the background or at one side. The terrace, which is quite lofty and overlooks the northern reaches of the Bay of Biscay, is paved with flagstones, partially surrounded by tamarisks, pines, and a crumbling stone balustrade. It might also be partially sheltered by a rough wooden roof or pavilion. There are sev-*

eral outdoor-type chairs and two or three stone benches drawn with rugs and furs. A small but sturdy wicker table sports a constant clutter of inkwells, pencil jars, boxes of paper, etc. A refreshment trolley, with a small liquor cabinet underneath, has been rolled out at one side.

Belle-Isle-en-Mer, an island off the coast of Brittany.

Les Poulains, SARAH BERNHARDT'S sprawling estate on the north point of the island.

The terrace of the manor house, Penhoët; a late afternoon in summer, 1922.

SARAH is dozing, propped up with cushions in a large wicker chair. She is seventy-seven years old. Seven and a half years before the time of the play, her right leg was amputated, several inches above the knee. Equipped with the latest thing in prostheses, she now perambulates cautiously but smoothly, supporting herself as necessary on companions and convenient pieces of furniture.

Music. SARAH stirs but does not appear to waken.

GEORGES PITOU enters from the house, sees SARAH. He is considerably younger than she, but with a balding monastic appearance and a professionally fatigued manner, in contrast to her customary nervous vigour. He creeps to her chair, notes her awkward slump. He touches her arm tentatively. She does not move. He stoops and, with great gentleness, lifts her artificial limb deftly by the instep, up a few inches, onto a low stool or cushion. He looks up. Her eyes are open. He straightens and fusses with his clothing, embarrassed. She stares at him thickly, half awake.]

SARAH: Pitou?...

PITOU: Who brought you out here? That's what I'd like to know. In this heat! That new fellow? Henri?

SARAH: This afternoon sun is like a fist, Pitou. There's not a breath of air. Look at the sea. White and silent as a punished child. Fetch my parasol.

PITOU: At once, Madame! Or probably you'd rather be taken inside? You know what Doctor Marot always says: a woman in your condition must be careful not to—

SARAH: Condition? What condition? My parasol!

PITOU: At once!

> *[He goes into the house. SARAH sits up, arranges her clothing, brushes the hair from her eyes, winces slightly, a fleeting pain. She looks out at the sun.]*

SARAH: Yes, I know. I know! I must ... accomplish something. Finally. But this heat—! Yes. You! You, too. Engaged in the agonizing process of consuming yourself, burning yourself to a cinder! Well—you won't be easy to replace.

> *[PITOU comes back in with embroidery on a frame. He brings it to SARAH.]*

SARAH: What's this?

PITOU: Your needlework, Madame.

SARAH: That's not what I asked for! *[throws it aside]*

PITOU: No? Are you sure?

SARAH: Parasol! My parasol! I'm dehydrating, Pitou! Like an old lizard.

PITOU: I knew it! Now you've got a fever!

SARAH: Nonsense! The sun!

PITOU: Who brought you out here? Encouraging your fever? Doctor Marot has tried to warn you—

SARAH: I do not have a fever! I want to—I must work!

PITOU: —in your condition even a slight fever can be indicative! Of something!

SARAH: Pitou—

PITOU: And of course I'll be blamed! "Pitou," you'll say, "it was Pitou who allowed me to sit out under the merciless August sun until—"

SARAH: Pitou! My parasol!

PITOU: At once. *[starts inside]*

SARAH: And bring the gramophone, too! Some music might jog me back into life.

PITOU: The gramophone? Here? Outside?

SARAH: Why not?

PITOU: The salt air, Madame! It corrodes all your little wheels, all your little cylinders, your little cogs!

SARAH: My little cogs?

PITOU: And music, Madame? Before supper? It's common medical knowledge that music irritates the digestive tract. My mother used to say to me, "The stomach and the ears are sympathetic organs, Georges. They should not be simultaneously required to—"

SARAH: *[thunders]* The gramophone!

PITOU: At once, Madame.

> *[He goes into the house. SARAH looks out at the sun.]*

SARAH: I have sworn to buy that poor fool a proper hairpiece! If, for just one day, he would not torture me with his babbling! With Doctor Marot's and his mother's medical opinions! But I know in my heart, he will go to his grave bald as an egg! *[pause]* Ah—damn! I should have asked him to bring the notes. Yes. Yes, I'll work! That will surprise Maurice. He will assume his pathetic parched old mother just lay here all afternoon, as usual. Like some parched old lizard under the sun's fist. *[grins]* My God—that's brilliant! Write it down, Pitou! Pitou? Where is he?

> *[PITOU comes back in, a small battered gramophone under one arm, an album of records under the other.]*

SARAH: Ah, Pitou! Write this down quickly! "To the world at large, I have become nothing more than a parched old—"

PITOU: Madame? Where do you want the—?

SARAH: Write, Pitou!

PITOU: Over here? *[staggers to a bench, puts down the gramophone, and records]*

SARAH: "I am nothing more than an old dehydrated lizard lying under the merciless fist—" Pitou! You're not writing this down!

PITOU: No, Madame.

SARAH: Why not?

PITOU: I'm not—I can't—I don't know what we're doing, Madame! I seldom do anymore.

SARAH: And where's my parasol?

PITOU: Your what?

SARAH: I distinctly requested my parasol!

PITOU: You distinctly requested the gramophone, Madame. Though I did try to warn you—

SARAH: And my parasol!

PITOU: *[smiles at her]* Obviously this heat—or an incipient fever—is playing tricks with one of our memories. The best thing for all concerned would be for us to drag ourselves inside and—

SARAH: Stop!

> *[She snatches a scrap of paper, scribbles on it. PITOU moves to her, looks over her shoulder.]*

SARAH: Now then. I have written "P–A–R–A—"

PITOU: I can read, Madame.

SARAH: Then fetch!

> *[She crams the scrap of paper into his hand. He starts out. She glances towards the sun.]*

SARAH: Ah! And bring the notes, too!

PITOU: The notes?

SARAH: The blue folder with the gillyflowers; you know where it is.

PITOU: The notes? Here, outside?

SARAH: And my parasol! And the notes in the blue folder!

PITOU: We're going to work on the Memoir? Out here?

SARAH: Why not?

PITOU: Then we won't need the gramophone! *[starts towards it]*

SARAH: Leave the gramophone, Pitou! Go away!

> *[He starts out.]*

SARAH: Pitou?...

PITOU: Madame?

SARAH: Where are you going?

PITOU: Inside, Madame.

SARAH: Why?

PITOU: You distinctly requested me to go away.

SARAH: And to fetch something, yes?

PITOU: Yes.

SARAH: The blue folder. Our notes for Volume Two of the Memoir.

SARAH: And?

PITOU: Madame?

SARAH: And?

> *[PITOU looks at her evenly, blankly.]*

SARAH: What's that in your hand, Pitou? In your left hand!

> *[PITOU looks at the paper she has scribbled on, unfolds*

it, and reads it, then looks back at her and sighs.]

PITOU: All right, then. Have it your own way. *[turns and goes into the house, his voice gradually fading]* But I simply fail to see how you can expect a parasol to bring relief from what is, quite obviously, a case of nervous dyspepesia aggravated by what started as an insignificant, but is now a rapidly accelerating, fever!...

[SARAH watches him go. Then she winces and touches her lower right side gingerly. She turns and looks out at the sun.]

SARAH: Yes. Why not? A little music. *[stands carefully and moves to the gramophone]* A melody by Mozart or Messager, to sting the memory awake. *[picks up the record album, flips through it]* Caruso?... Scotti?... Nellie Melba? God, no. She sings like every Australian. All the notes but none of the music!... Caruso again ... Alma Gluck? That one is cracked!... Geraldine Farrar? Definitely not!... Miss Mary Garden? Yes! *[takes the record from the album]* Yes, Miss Garden. You sing from the soul. *[puts the record on the gramophone]* No, from the belly! Which is even better!

[She starts the record. Music: Mary Garden sings "L'amour est une ⟨vertu⟩ rare" from Thaïs]

a characteristic quality in French

SARAH: Yes ... yes, Miss Garden! Gently. Lest you make her angry. Make her even angrier than she already is. She knows, Miss Garden. She knows that her days, her hours, her very months are numbered! And so every second now must count—must be an accomplishment! Though it consumes the little light, the precious little fire she still has left!

[She closes her eyes, sways to the music. After a moment, she smiles. PITOU comes back in with a large messy folder of notes.]

PITOU: Madame?

SARAH: Sshh!

PITOU: Madame, our notes!

SARAH: Gently. The music. The sun!

PITOU: The notes!

SARAH: Quiet! *[pause—resumes her swaying]*

PITOU: *[loud]* I thought we intended to work!

SARAH: I am, Pitou! I am remembering! Remembering my mother!

PITOU: Your mother?

SARAH: My mother—!

PITOU: One moment, Madame! *[sits and paws through the blue folder]*

SARAH: My mother, Judith van Haard, was the daughter of a Dutch Jew who made straw furniture. But she was ambitious. By the time she was twenty, she had become French, Catholic, and a kept woman.

PITOU: We put all that in your first volume, Madame.

SARAH: A very well kept woman! She bought herself a better life with her beauty, her refined manner, and her special amatory skills. I inherited none of these. And that broke her heart. I am assuming she had one.

PITOU: Here she is! "Mother!" *[waves a sheaf of notes]*

SARAH: To the world at large my mother appeared to be—

PITOU: "Mother," filed under "P" for "Parent."

SARAH: —my mother was like a bunch of violets!

PITOU: Subfiled under "M," of course.

SARAH: A fragile bouquet of imported Dutch violets—

PITOU: For "Maternal."

SARAH: —which have changed hands so often they are no longer quite fresh.

PITOU: "Parent," semicolon, "Maternal."

SARAH: But the chafing of all those hands has heightened their perfume!

PITOU: i.e., "Mother."

SARAH: Pitou! You're not writing this down?

PITOU: At once! *[grabs paper and pencil, scribbles]*

SARAH: My mother was like dried violets from Holland. Their fragrance is most powerful when they have been crushed a little.

PITOU: A bit slower, Madame?

SARAH: That's how she seemed! But beneath their gown of gauze and tissue paper, the violets had tendrils of steel, thorns much nastier than any outsider could have—. The record has stopped, Pitou.

PITOU: Thank God.

SARAH: Start it again.

PITOU: But, Madame—

SARAH: Start it again.

PITOU: You and Miss Garden at the same time? I'm only human.

SARAH: Don't exaggerate. Start the record again.

[She looks out at the sun. PITOU moves wearily to the gramophone.]

PITOU: In any case, we didn't leave off with her. Your mother, I mean. That's not what we were doing last time. We were doing South America. Remember? Brazil, Argentina, eighteen-ninety—ninety-something?

SARAH: *[gesturing imperiously]* Miss Garden!

> *[PITOU starts the record again: Mary Garden, as before. SARAH looks out at the sun, winces slightly.]*

PITOU: *[prompting]* From "violets," Madame?

SARAH: No....

PITOU: From "dried violets"?

SARAH: No.... God!... It's no use!

PITOU: From something about "dried Dutch violets"?

SARAH: It's—no!—it's not going to work!

PITOU: Yes, yes, it was something about your mother and dried violets and a ball gown. Your mother always wore violets, was that it? From her homeland? Or tried to grow them? She tried to grow violets with little thorns, so as to protect their freshness, was that it? Actually, Madame, I'm not quite sure what it was you were trying to—

SARAH: It's—not—going—to—work!

> *[She tears the record from the gramophone and smashes it angrily, then stares at PITOU as though he'd done it. Pause.]*

PITOU: Poor Miss Garden. She sings flat, it's true, but that's no reason to—

SARAH: Forget Miss Garden.

PITOU: And I suppose we'll have to buy another needle for the—

SARAH: Forget the needle! Pitou, I must work this afternoon. But my brain, this simmering pot, refuses to come to the boil!

PITOU: I'll fetch Doctor Marot.

SARAH: No! There's only one medicine, only one cure for my fever! Doctors are all fools, or worse, as I've told you before! You—you, Pitou, must help me! Minister to me!

PITOU: Yes, I'll help you inside, Madame, and then—

SARAH: No! Look at me. You know, don't you? You know what's to be done.

PITOU: Madame, I can't! Please?

SARAH: It always helps. It usually helps. Look at what we were able to accomplish last time for Brazil and Argentina. You were hired to help me!

PITOU: But not—why can't we just relax for the remainder of the afternoon? Tomorrow morning we can make a fresh start.

SARAH: Tomorrow morning is a chronological illusion! The sun has been reduced to an angry ember! There is only this afternoon!

PITOU: I ... I can't!

SARAH: So! You don't really care about the Memoir!

PITOU: I don't—? It was my idea! A second volume of Madame's recollections. For the enlightenment of the civilized world. And America.

SARAH: Come along, then. It always helps. You, you Pitou, this merciless afternoon, you shall be—my mother! Nagging, scolding, whining, you do it so well.

PITOU: I'm not an actor!

SARAH: The sun will flicker and then fade away forever! But the pot will boil first! The old lizard will dance round the dying embers! Maurice and the civilized world will be astonished!

PITOU: *[a last-ditch attempt]* There is absolutely nothing in my contract obliging me to indulge Madame in these perverse games. I pointed that fact out the very first time you suggested it, but obviously it is necessary, at the present time, to reiterate—

SARAH: Pitou, you will do it! *[pause; she looks directly into him]* You—will—do—it.

   [Pause.]

PITOU: How do we start?

   [SARAH looks out at the sun. Pause.]

SARAH: I am twenty-seven years old.

PITOU: *[starts to protest; thinks better of it]* Whatever you say.

SARAH: I am living in a drab little paradise on the Left Bank. With my lover, the Prince Henri de Ligne. And our darling little baby, our little Maurice—. Where is Maurice, by the way?

PITOU: Down at the cove with Doctor Marot and your granddaughter. Fishing for shrimp.

SARAH: Excellent! We won't be interrupted! Quiet!

   [PITOU doesn't move a muscle. Pause.]

I am twenty-seven and almost happy. Until I receive a visit from my exquisitely beautiful, exquisitely cruel mother. *[turns on Pitou]* From you! You've come to nag and scold and whine, I suppose? And to perform the rest of the standard maternal repertoire?

[PITOU starts to speak.]

Oh, yes, I know, Maman! I am a hideous disappointment! You are one of the most glamourous and successful women in Paris, in France, which is to say, in the world! I've heard your self-congratulatory aria so often! You have achieved affluence, Maman, and even—respectability?—by taking to bed with you all the most influential men in the country. One at a time, usually.

PITOU: Madame—

SARAH: Please! It's "Mademoiselle." I'm no more married than you have ever been, Maman.

PITOU: Madame, I really can't—I can't possibly pretend—

SARAH: You can, you can, Pitou! You're more gifted than you think! And besides, it's only a game! A game to jog my flickering memory under this merciless sun! Without even a parasol!

PITOU: A parasol, Madame? You need only ask! *[starts out]*

SARAH: Pitou! Georges?

[He stops.]

Don't! Don't make this too difficult for me. Georges. Please?...

[Pause.]

PITOU: How do we start?

SARAH: You start. Maman always started.

PITOU: But what should I—?

SARAH: Please don't whine! You are Judith Bernhardt. One of the most ...

PITOU: Glamourous?

SARAH: ... and successful?...

PITOU: Women in Paris.

SARAH: Exactly!

> [*Pause.* PITOU *turns away from her, trying to "get into the role." He picks up a small ornamental fan, a "character prop," then suddenly turns back to her.*]

PITOU: [*as Judith Bernhardt*] Now then, Mademoiselle Sarah—!

SARAH: Now then, Maman?

PITOU: [*Judith*] Don't call me that! You must be twenty-seven years old!

SARAH: Twenty-six.

PITOU: Twenty—? Are you sure?

SARAH: Get on with it.

PITOU: [*Judith*] You must be twenty-six years old. Surely it's time you left the theatre, to seek honest employment!

SARAH: Splendid, Pitou—. My life is no one's business but mine, Maman. My life is my only actual possession!

PITOU: [*Judith*] And you are more than welcome to it! But what about—? What about...?

SARAH: *[prompting]* What about my baby?

PITOU: *[Judith]* What about this sickly little baby? And what about...?

SARAH: Prince Henri?

PITOU: *[Judith]* Yes! This fly-by-night Belgian dandy! I assume he's actually the father of your little bastard?

SARAH: Maman! Prince Henri adores me—

PITOU: *[Judith]* Oh, the nobility's always game for a quick backstage tumble, dear! He'll sing a different tune when his parents discover a smear of greasepaint on the family crest.

SARAH: Bravo, Pitou—! Go on, Maman. You know what comes next. "I spent my youth, ruined my health—"

PITOU: I know, I know! Don't rush me. *[Judith]* I spent my youth, ruined my health to give my two daughters a decent life!

SARAH: Oh, be honest! For once in your life, Maman! Whatever you spent or ruined, it was for Jeanne, not for me. For Jeanne!

PITOU: *[Judith]* Well, why not? Jeanne never abused me, defied me, as you have done all your life! Jeanne required more attention, more care. You were strong enough. Too strong! Jeanne doesn't have your temperament, thank God, or your obscene selfishness!

SARAH: *[laughs]* You can't tell me you're not enjoying this, Pitou!

PITOU: Madame! How can I possibly continue this charade if you distract and interrupt at every—?

SARAH: I'm sorry, I'm sorry—? Go on, Maman. Go on!

PITOU: *[Judith]* You, Sarah, you are the altar of thorns on which my heart first bled. And on which it has bled ever since! If only you had respected me, listened to me—

SARAH: You wanted Jeanne and me to be perfect replicas of yourself, didn't you, Maman? A Dresden china bitch and her two china whelps!

PITOU: *[Judith]* Mademoiselle! I'll thank you to remember to whom you are speaking! You might at least—in this heat—offer your mother a little refreshment!

SARAH: *[smiles]* Help yourself, Maman.

> *[PITOU hurries to the refreshment trolley and helps himself to sherry or some other restorative.]*

PITOU: And you?...

SARAH: No, thank you, Maman.

PITOU: *[sips and fans, as Judith]* Yes. Yes, Sarah. If Paris, which is to say the world, has sometimes been amused by your tantrums, onstage and off—I have not! Virtually from birth you were self-willed, impractical! Prey to the most absurd fantasies about yourself—

SARAH: Maman—

PITOU: *[Judith]* About life, about men! Even when I managed to dig up highly eligible suitors for you, which was no easy task considering—

SARAH: Highly eligible? When I was barely fifteen you tried to saddle me with that hairy mammoth, the hirsute Monsieur Berentz! I'd never seen a man, I'd never seen an animal so unalterably corporeal! Bristly! He even had hair growing under his fingernails!

PITOU: *[Judith]* He had a fine business.

SARAH: Yes! He made rugs! From his own hair, no doubt!

PITOU: *[as Judith, sighs and turns away from her]* Doctors customarily advise mature women to avoid alcohol, rich food, and any prolonged exercise which might injure the spine. My doctors simply advised me to avoid my elder daughter!

SARAH: That's it, Maman. Say what you came here to say, sing the whole piece! How you suffered, how you sacrificed—

PITOU: *[Judith]* How I—! Well, what mother would not suffer? I watched, helpless, as my little Sarah evolved into a shrill rebellious creature with a harsh Semitic profile—not entirely her fault, I suppose—and with an avid affectation for the theatre and all its infectious filth! *[turns on her]* Yes, infectious! It wasn't bad enough to throw away your own life and self-respect! You had to drag my whole family after you! You had to introduce my poor little Jeanne, my baby, my angel, to your theatrical poison! To a passion and a vulgarity she was not strong enough to resist, much less sustain—!

SARAH: Stop! Stop now! *[gestures vaguely, desperately towards paper and pencil]*

> *[PITOU understands, abandons the role of Judith, and hurries to the blue folder. He takes out paper, sits, and prepares to scribble. SARAH looks out at the sun.]*

Yes! Yes, I know! She was—is—so angry! How she suffered. Sacrificed! But for Jeanne. Always, only for Jeanne! My sister, Jeanne, my mother's good angel, would suddenly say to me, "Sarah, there's a carousel behind my eyes!" And I'd know she was blind drunk again. Maman blamed me. "Your sister never drank before you dragged her off on your insane insatiable tours! To New York and God knows where else!" The truth is, I didn't want to drag Jeanne along. But she whined and wheedled. She said I was jealous, I was afraid she might show me up to the Americans. Because she was younger and so much more beautiful. So I dragged her along. I gave her a few little speeches to recite, a few wigs and frocks to dress up in. Taught her to mask the sleepless eyes and ragged cheeks with paint. But I did not teach her to drink, Maman! I have always despised that weakness, that self-ishness! In anyone! It may be true that I ... looked the other way. Yes, perhaps I let it happen. Perhaps I was glad it happened. Because I unquestionably hated her, hated my sister Jeanne! Virtually from birth! But who infected me with that, Maman? Who saw to it that Jeanne was always given the finest clothes, the holidays by the sea, the facial massages with fresh cream? You taught Jeanne how to be beautiful, while drilling me in the arts of household management! Of course I grew up determined to be totally impractical! And enormously desirable! Of course I went into the theatre! I fought my way into the Conservatoire and fought to stay there, Maman, while you sighed and sneered. You and your elegant sneering gentlemen. You blushed every time my name was mentioned. Because, unlike Jeanne, I had no real possibilities. That's what you told me, over and over again: "Sarah, I know you're a clever girl, but you have no real possibilities." Whereas Jeanne—I always wondered who her father was!—had at least the possibility of being poured into your porcelain mould, Maman! "You can look like a Jew, Sarah, and be beautiful," you used to say to me, "or you can look like a Jew and look like a Jew." Jeanne was so beautiful. For a little while. Jeanne had a nose that was just a nose. Jeanne had a mouth. She had hair. I had only my eyes. Everything else I had to invent! Yes! Because the public—like you, Maman—the terrible public demands beauty! A smooth skin, a perfect mouth, a generous breast with veins of luminous blue like Italian marble! Or at least the appearance, the vivid impression of those things! And I have served the public, Maman, according to its appetite! I have fed it, fed it my health, my heart, my constantly re-invented old flesh! Haven't I, Maman—? Haven't I, Pitou?

PITOU: *[looks up from his frantic scribbling]* Which am I?

SARAH: *[looks at him; pause]* Pitou.

PITOU: *[riffles through the blue folder and extracts a page from which he reads]* "For more than fifty years la Bernhardt has given the people of this world the vibrations of her soul, the pulse of her heart, the tears of her eyes, performing more than one hundred and twenty-five different roles with uncompromising—"

SARAH: Stop! Stop, Pitou! What is that drivel? Makes me sound like a national monument.

PITOU: I am quoting Madame herself.

SARAH: Never! That—that cadenza about vibrations and—? I said that?

PITOU: Word for word. Just last week. "Seventh of August, 1922." I filed it under "P." For "Prolonged Digressions."

SARAH: Well ... I am less of a fool this week than last. File that under "P." For "Progress." *[slight pause; turns and looks out at the sun]* But, Pitou, you're straying from the path again! Where were we? South America?

PITOU: Madame, it's nearly time for supper.

SARAH: I'm not hungry.

PITOU: I am.

SARAH: No, not for food! I must—yes, a little further. Please. A little more today. *[turns to him]* Start again. Pitou. Maman?

PITOU: God save me.

SARAH: Don't whine. We must accomplish something! You were exquisite as my mother. Except for that ink smudge on your chin. That is definitely out of character.

[PITOU turns away, rubs his chin violently.]

Oh, God, now I've wounded you again! I'm sorry. Oh, Pitou, you're exactly like one of those—those little creatures we always find on the beach at low tide. Doctor Marot assures me they have no nervous system, none at all. But the moment I touch them, or even come near, they shriek and wriggle and change colour. *[pause]* I do love you, Pitou.

PITOU: Thank you, Madame. I know.

SARAH: Excellent. So. We'll start again. Maman? You were saying?...

> *[PITOU appeals to her with his eyes. She stares back, inflexible.]*

You were saying, Maman?!

PITOU: *[wilts; perfunctorily picks up the fan again; as Judith Bernhardt]* Now then, Sarah, you are twenty-six years old—and, as I was saying—

SARAH: No, no! I am eleven!

PITOU: Eleven?

SARAH: Play along, Pitou, play along!

PITOU: But you've never been eleven, Madame! I haven't the faintest idea how to—

SARAH: Oh, my mother was the same, whatever her age! I am eleven now. You are twenty-six, Maman.

PITOU: *[thinking this over; struggling]* I became a mother at a very tender age!

SARAH: We are standing, my mother and I, before a grey wall, which disappears into grey trees which disappear into a grey sky. Maman has brought me to the convent at Grand-Champs. She is handing me over to the nuns for domestication. She can't endure my ugliness anymore, or my bad manners. I squeeze and tickle all her gentlemen friends. In places where gentlemen friends should not be squeezed or tickled. She is abandoning me! I am sobbing my heart out! *[puts one hand over her eyes and sobs like a child]* But I can still hear my implacable mother! She is chatting with Mère Sainte Sophie, the Superior of the convent. Yes, yes, I can hear her— *[turns on PITOU]* chatting!

PITOU: Chatting about what? We've never done anything like this before! I haven't the faintest idea what to—

SARAH: Oh, all right, all right! You make everything so difficult! You were hired to help me, but you refuse to make use of the mind, the imagination, the nervous system, which God, all evidence to the contrary, must have given, even to you! *[catches her breath]* All right. You are no longer my mother.

PITOU: Thank God.

SARAH: You are Mère Sainte Sophie of the convent at Grand-Champs.

PITOU: Oh, no!

SARAH: Here. Put on this shawl.

PITOU: No!

> *[SARAH drapes the shawl over his head and shoulders.]*

This is just not right.

SARAH: There. Lovely.

PITOU: Why can't I ever be a man?

SARAH: In the convent?

PITOU: The gardener? The postman!

SARAH: Mère Sainte Sophie! Divine! And she had a slight limp, I remember. A sort of ethereal limp.

PITOU: Can't I just be your mother again?

SARAH: *[takes the fan from him]* Too late! Maman is gone! In her enormous black phaeton. Listen! There it goes, rattling across the cobblestones in the convent courtyard! I am little Sarah Bernhardt, eleven years old and frightened to death. Weeping in a dark corner. You are a tall grey woman with a limp and a voice like a clay jug thrown against a stone wall. You want to comfort and console me. Everything familiar to me on this earth has vanished in that black phaeton! You take my trembling little hand in your enormous rough grey one. *[seizes PITOU'S hand]* You speak to me. *[resumes sobbing]*

PITOU: *[very reluctantly, as Mère Sainte Sophie]* Mademoiselle Bernhardt. You are eleven years old—

SARAH: *[drops his hand; irritably]* Mary, Mother of God!

PITOU: Madame?

SARAH: Must you start every scene with the same old expository dialogue? "Mademoiselle, you are so many years old." It's worse than Sardou!

PITOU: I don't claim to be a dramatist!

SARAH: But we're supposed to be human beings! People! People do not commence every conversation by announcing the age of their listeners! You must have noticed that, Pitou! What would Mère Sainte Sophie say, under the given circumstances, at the given time?

PITOU: I don't really know any nuns.

SARAH: Think! Start again.

PITOU: I'm doing my best.

SARAH: Well, do better! Start again. Here I am, eleven years old, weeping in a dark corner. Comfort me, Reverend Mother! Speak to me. *[turns away again, sobs]*

PITOU: *[approaching nervously, as Mère Sainte Sophie]* Mademoiselle Sarah?...

SARAH: Yes? What is it?

PITOU: *[Mère Sainte Sophie]* Mademoiselle Sarah, you are—you are weeping in a dark corner, I see—

> *[SARAH turns on him, glaring, furious. He throws off the shawl, moves away.]*

All right, all right! I'm hopeless! It's all hopeless! I give up!!

SARAH: *[continues glaring; a painful pause]* Very—well—then. I give up, too! Why not? Take it all away! Destroy it! Yes, burn it all!

> *[She takes handfuls of notes from the blue folder, scatters them furiously about. PITOU doesn't dare stop her.]*

PITOU: No!

SARAH: You were hired to help me! I cannot do it alone! Why did we ever start?! Why did you persuade me to try? What use is it all? Press clippings, citations, invitations, this specimen collection of my life! It's ludicrous! Laughable!

PITOU: *[at the same time]* No! Please! Stop!

SARAH: I know, I know! This is what you want! What all of you want! For me to just lie here like some helpless mutilated old lizard!

PITOU: Stop! Stop!

SARAH: *[at the same time]* While the little light, the little heat, which I still have left drains out of me! You want me to lie still and welcome the cold and the darkness!

PITOU: *[picks up the small fan again and raps on the table with it, trying to drown her out]* Stop, stop, stop!

SARAH: *[at the same time]* But no! No! That is my answer to all of you! I will not give up! I must and will do—say—mean something! Yes! Yes! Yes!

PITOU: *[at the same time]* Stop! Stop! Stop! Stop, stop, stop!...

> *[He continues shouting and rapping with the fan for a moment after SARAH has grown silent. Then he realizes. He looks at her, then looks at the fan, which is in tatters. Pause.]*

SARAH: That fan. Was presented to me, Pitou. At the Trocadero Gardens during the Universal Exhibition of 1878. By the Emperor of Ceylon. *[pause]* It was fashioned of hand-woven silk and precious monkey bones. It took thirty-two Buddhist priests more than three years to complete the intricate design. Thirty-two! Thousands of days and nights, carving, staining, painting, polishing. Pausing only to pray or to fast, to renew their inspiration. Then back to their carving, staining, painting, polishing. And so on.

> *[Pause. PITOU lays the fan down carefully, then stoops and retrieves the notes SARAH has scattered. He returns them to the blue folder on the table.]*

PITOU: This heat. This dry wind. This wretched island. My mother always warned me about a coastal climate. I've had a terrible week. My kidneys—

SARAH: The priests of Ceylon should not have to answer for your kidneys! Nor should I.

> *[Pause.]*

PITOU: Right. So I'll be Mère Saint Sophie, tall and grey, and you'll be—

SARAH: No. I'm going to close my eyes. Just for a moment.

PITOU: Ah. Good idea. We'll go inside and—

SARAH: No! Just for a moment.

PITOU: Right. Shall I start the gramophone again?

SARAH: *[shakes her head, "No"]* But I would love to have my parasol.

PITOU: At once. *[starts out]*

SARAH: Yes, she knows she's dying.

PITOU: Madame—?

SARAH: That peevish old August sun. She'll be extinct. In a mere billion or trillion years. I think she's punishing us, don't you? She's sulking, the old bitch. Terribly disappointed to discover she's not, after all, immortal.

> *[Pause.]*

PITOU: And perhaps a cool drink, Madame?

SARAH: Yes. Wonderful. Run along now. I'll just rest my eyes until you get back.

> *[PITOU goes quickly into the house. SARAH opens her eyes and looks out at the sun. After a moment, she shakes her head sharply, as though to wake herself up. She reaches for the blue folder of notes, pulls it into her lap, and thumbs through it.]*

How in God's name can he find anything in here? Everything, everything is filed under "P"! "Productions," "Post Cards," "Parents," "Profanity"! The tatters and treasures of my endless life. Pitou needs only one consonant to classify them all! "Premières"—*[takes a tattered theatrical programme from the folder]*

Comédie Française—*The Marriage of Figaro*—January, 1873. My God, the Ice Age! Was I alive then? *[thumbs through the folder]* *Cleopatra. Fédora. Froufrou. Hernani*—*[suddenly snatches another old programme from the folder]* *Phaedra!* *[holds the programme up in the air, proudly out towards the sun]* You see this? You remember?— Oh, yes, you do! *[lowers the programme, looks at it]* December, 1874. *Phaedra.* All Paris, which is to say the world, held its breath. Stopped breathing, stopped blinking, stopped thinking. Lived and desired and died with me, with me alone, for two and a half hours. Which is to say, forever. *[looks out at the sun, winces slightly, then suddenly crams the programme back into the folder; takes a deep unsteady breath]* And now? Now I play children's games. With Pitou. Pitou—with his face which someone scrawled on a chalkboard—with fingernails that haven't been trimmed since his confirmation! Two grimy exhausted children. And all the others, too, even Maurice. They all play games with me. Games to amuse the ancient child, now that her life, her heat, her light is almost spent. Now that she slides, every day, a little deeper into the earth. The mud. The darkness. Every day, every moment, deeper. And so feebly. So quietly, so tamely! Not a cry, not a sound. Except the exhausted old flesh as it sighs and unfolds and comes apart. The old claws as they crackle and snatch and strain to keep a grip on something—anything!—that is sharp and solid. *[pause]* And then even the crackling fades. The flesh become the mud and the darkness. And someone passing by says, "Oh, look, once there was a fire here."

> *[She looks out at the sun, then closes her eyes tightly and slumps back in her chair. After a moment PITOU comes back in with a parasol. He sees SARAH'S awkward slump and hurries to her.]*

PITOU: Madame? *[touches her arm]* Madame—?

> *[SARAH opens her eyes and smiles at him.]*

Your parasol, Madame.

SARAH: *[takes the parasol and immediately puts it aside]* And my cool drink?

PITOU: Cool drink? Madame distinctly requested—but what a good idea! We'll go inside, and I'll have the kitchen send something cool up to your—

SARAH: No! Never mind. It's late, it's getting cooler out here.

PITOU: Is it?

SARAH: Where were we? The Comédie Française? *Phaedra!*

PITOU: Oh, no, I don't think so. *[sits, studies his notes]*

SARAH: *[reviving]* December, eighteen-seventy-something?

PITOU: Actually I fear we'd wandered even farther afield than that. I did try to point out that a little organization would not be—

SARAH: *[suddenly cries out, as Phaedra]* "Then we'll go no farther!"

PITOU: *[looks up, confused]* You mean, this afternoon? What a good idea!

SARAH: *[Phaedra]* "Stay and rest!"

PITOU: Absolutely, Madame! We'll just creep quietly inside and—

SARAH: *[Phaedra]*
"I cannot move, Oenone! I am possessed!
My eyes are blistered by the light of day!
I faint, I fall, my trembling knees give way!
Alas!"

[Struggles with her apparel, as Phaedra.]

PITOU: *[realizing what she's up to]* Alas.

SARAH: *[Phaedra]*
"How heavy are these gems, this crown, these veils!
They drag me down! And what conniving hand

Has bound my forehead with this scarlet band?
Yes, all of you conspire to hurt and mock me!"

   [Glances at PITOU, then looks out at the sun.]

"You shining author of my tragic race!
My mother called you 'Father' to your face,
That burnished face which now must blush to see
My shame, my shame, my shame eternally!"
—Pitou!

   [PITOU looks up from his notes.]

You're not listening!

PITOU: I've heard Madame's Phaedra a thousand times.

SARAH: The scene is new every time I do it!

PITOU: Yes, but Madame knows my opinion of the so-called "classics." Racine, Corneille—whoever! They didn't write about real people.

SARAH: No?

PITOU: No! Grown women, panting like draft horses, throwing themselves at men's feet! Writhing. Perspiring!

SARAH: No one ever writhed and perspired over you?

PITOU: I'm proud to say no one ever did.

SARAH: But you—you, Pitou? Didn't you ever heave and groan and pop your button?

PITOU: Pop my—?

SARAH: You told me—I remember—you were desperately in love, once upon a time.

PITOU: Maybe. Once upon a time.

SARAH: Yes, yes, you told me all about—what was her name again?

PITOU: I don't remember.

SARAH: Liar. Wait a minute ... Lisette! That was it!

PITOU: Was it?

SARAH: Yes, little Lisette! You were all set to be married, but some-how it didn't work out.

PITOU: You seem to know the story better than I do.

SARAH: Why didn't it work out?

PITOU: Why are you doing this, Madame? It's an intensely personal matter. I am not required by my contract to discuss—

SARAH: *[abruptly assuming a girlish tilt of the head and the piping voice of a young peasant]* Oh, please, Georges! Please? Why can't we be married? Right away? What's wrong, Georges? Have you found someone else? Don't you love your little Lisette anymore?

PITOU: Don't do this.

SARAH: *[Lisette]* I promise to treasure you all my life, Georges! I promise to scrub the floors and the children's faces and your lovely strong back when you come home from—!

PITOU: Stop it!

[Startled by his fierceness, SARAH stops, stares at him.]

[quietly] It wasn't like that. Not at all. She wasn't like that.

SARAH: You've been so selfish with that part of your life, what could I do? I was improvising—

PITOU: *[strongly, but not loud]* Well, I don't want you to improvise! Not with my life. Accuracy matters to some of us, you see. Not merely the emotion and the spectacle. But the facts.

SARAH: The facts?...

> *[He looks at SARAH. She is looking at him, evenly, demandingly. Music. PITOU turns away from her again, to tell his story.]*

PITOU: *[after a considerable pause; very quietly]* I was only twenty-five years old. She was only twenty-four. We were perfect together. Everyone said so. Her father made bread and mine made cheese. We'd been engaged since we were children. "Georges and Lisette," people used to say. "It's inevitable." Unfortunately they were wrong.

SARAH: *[very softly]* Why?

PITOU: There was no "Please, Georges, I promise to treasure you!" Lisette was a sensitive highly intelligent girl. Which was the heart of the problem, in a sense. *[pause]* The fact is ... it was a very hot day. Lisette's parents had gone for an outing in the country. She'd planned it that way, but I didn't realize. I just stopped by to say hello. I always stopped by on my way home from work, but that day—she was all alone. And it was unseasonably hot for April. *[pause]* We sat in her parent's garden. In the arbor—grapevines hanging down all around, tickling the back of my neck. Lisette looked at me. I already knew what she was going to say. "Where's the harm, Georges? In a few weeks, we'll be married, and what I'm asking you to do will be perfectly legal, perfectly sacred. Why not today, Georges? Don't you want to?" Of course I wanted to! But it still seemed wrong. "It's not a question of morality, Lisette, but of personality! Some people don't need the priest and the hymns and the flowers on the altar, but we do! At least, I do. I have a sense of tradition, a sense of order!" I confess, I sounded a bit silly, even to myself. *[pause]*

SARAH: *[even more softly]* Yes?

PITOU: *[after a moment, still looking away]* Lisette took me by the hand and led me to a grove of lime trees at the end of the garden. It was darker there and terribly hot. Little beads of water stood out all over her face. *[pause]* She began to undress, very slowly, very seriously. She folded each article of clothing and hung it on the limb of a tree. What could I do? I wanted her to know that I wanted her. Just as much as she wanted—so I followed suit. *[pause]* It was perfectly still, except for the locusts. We turned to face each other. *[pause]* And then. Lisette began to laugh.

SARAH: *[puzzled]* To laugh?

PITOU: Not shyly. Not nervously. Gleefully! Hysterically! I kept saying, "What's wrong, Lisette? What's so damned funny?" But she was laughing too hard to answer!

SARAH: You mean—Pitou—she was laughing at you?

[He says nothing, looks out at the sun. Pause.]

[quietly, genuinely] My God, Pitou, what agony!

PITOU: And she just kept on laughing! My embarrassment soon turned to anger. I could have strangled her! Instead I got dressed again. And I left. Her laughter, still ringing in my ears!...

[Pause.]

SARAH: And you never saw little Lisette again?

PITOU: Only once. When she came by to say she was breaking off the engagement.

SARAH: Oh, no.

PITOU: "Georges," she said, "I had never seen a man before. I mean, an entire man. I never even thought about it really."

SARAH: A-ha.

PITOU: "It's not your fault, Georges," she said, "but, now that I have seen what a man is, I just don't see how I could ever take marriage seriously."

   [SARAH smiles to herself, almost laughs.]

And I could see she was about to burst out laughing, all over again!

   [SARAH suppresses her smile.]

Years later, I ran into somebody from home who told me Lisette became an illustrator of children's stories.

   [SARAH quickly suppresses another smile, then stretches out her hand to PITOU.]

SARAH: It's an amazing story, Georges.

   [PITOU turns and looks at her, then moves to take her hand.]

A touching true story. About real people.

PITOU: I suppose so.

SARAH: No, I really am deeply touched! Oh, I know, the world at large thinks that I have no human feelings left! That I'm just a half-dead old dragon, licking my wounds and— *[looking past him]* Pitou! The sun is going down!

PITOU: Yes, it usually does. At night.

SARAH: But no! It's not necessarily going down. Somewhere it is rising again!

PITOU: Couldn't we go inside now?

SARAH: In Japan or Manchuria!

PITOU: I really am quite hungry.

SARAH: The sun is a relative of mine, you know. Half the world is forever dozing but not the sun, and not me! We don't require sleep. We don't dare!

PITOU: I could fix a nice pot of herb tea?

SARAH: *[fiercely shaking her head, "No"]* Accomplish! Something! I dare not close my eyes. I may never open them again. Well, not upon this world!

PITOU: *[a deep tired sigh]* Just as you say, Madame. *[glances at his notes] Phaedra?*

SARAH: No, no—! America!

PITOU: America? Before supper?

SARAH: America! The dust and the dollars! *[laughs]*

PITOU: Alas.

SARAH: *[at the same time]* New York, Virginia, Texas, California. Indians!

PITOU: Indians?

SARAH: Locomotives!

PITOU: *[a desperate whisper]* Locomotives!... *[sits, resigned, and scribbles as she speaks]*

SARAH: Somewhere ... in an American railway car ... bridges and tunnels and stars! The rest of my little troupe has gone to sleep hours ago. Even poor sister Jeanne, with a bottle of gin cradled in her arms like a doll. The terrible Mister Jarrett, my terrible manager, has told us in his terrible voice: "You bloody god-damned people need your bloody goddamned rest! Go to bed, goddamnit!" But I cannot rest. There is someone in bed beside me. But I don't remember which one it is. Doesn't matter! I am sitting, naked as Eve the first night in Eden, watching, as the lights from miniature towns and miniature horses stop to watch as Miss Sarah Bernhardt's private railway car clatters past in the dust or the snow. *[American accent]* "Oh, yeah! Sarah Bernhardt! Oldest woman in the world! Came over here and got away with more loot than Billy the Kid!"

> *[PITOU smiles, continues scribbling. It grows darker.]*

America! President Wilson ... President Roosevelt ... President McKinley. They shot him, and he had such a gentle face. My chats with the electrifying Mister Thomas Edison—all about Shakespeare and the other forces of Nature! And of course Marguerite Gauthier, "Our Lady of the Camellias." God, how the Americans loved to watch that woman die! "Camille," they called her. I tried to tell them, "Camille is a man's name!" That didn't seem to bother the Americans.

PITOU: *[more or less to himself, disdainfully]* Americans!...

SARAH: The terrible Mister Jarrett used to call it my "piggy bank role." Whenever, wherever poor Marguerite's lungs finally gave out, there was always a full house to witness her demise!

> *[She closes her eyes, takes several quick shallow breaths, clasps her lower right side with one hand. PITOU stops scribbling, looks up.]*

PITOU: Madame?...

SARAH: *[as Marguerite Gauthier]* "Is that you, Armand?... Speak to me, my darling. Say something."

> *[PITOU reluctantly sits near her. She takes his hand and clasps it to her breast.]*

[Marguerite] "All these months while you were away, Armand—I was so angry with Death! But now Death and I can be friends again. Because he allows me these last few precious moments with you. With you—the only one that I ever really loved! Yes, the pure and generous Marguerite, who was reborn in your arms, will live forever in your memory, Armand. But she inhabited the body of a sinful exhausted woman. And now that woman is dying. Which is as it should be. Do you understand? Tell me that you understand!"

[Closes her eyes, clasps his hand even more tightly.]

PITOU: *[as Armand Duval, improvising]* "Yes. Yes, Marguerite, I understand."

SARAH: *[Marguerite; after a considerable pause, takes a deep breath, then smiles]* "Oh ... how strange!"

PITOU: What?

SARAH: *[Marguerite]* "Suddenly all the pain is gone!" *[opens her eyes and looks out at the fading sun]* "It is surely a miracle! I feel—well again! I feel better—better than I ever felt in all my life! Oh, my dearest Armand! I shall live!"

[Smiling ecstatically, she releases PITOU'S hand. Then suddenly she shudders, closes her eyes tightly, and one hand rises spasmodically, clutching the air repeatedly. Then, a long frozen stillness. SARAH suddenly relaxes and falls back, limp, into her chair. PITOU stares at her for a long moment.]

PITOU: "Rest in peace, dear Marguerite. Much will be forgiven you, for you have loved so much." *[another brief pause; as himself]* Phhhft! Curtain! The crowd goes wild!

[Without sitting up, SARAH opens her eyes and smiles.]

Bravo, Madame.

SARAH: Bravo, Pitou! You even remembered Nichette's little curtain speech!

PITOU: *[grinning]* Well, I don't know if Madame recalls: once in—Kansas City, I think it was—Madame's sister was "indisposed"? For a while we thought I might have to put on a wig and play Nichette!

SARAH: *[sits up, laughing]* Oh, yes, Madame recalls! I spent all afternoon pouring foul black American coffee down the stupid girl's throat! In order to spare an unsuspecting public your acting debut!

PITOU: *[stands, offended, and moves back to his notes]* I never claimed to be an actor! You're the one who forces me into these ridiculous—

SARAH: *[looking out to sea]* Dear God, Pitou! It's getting quite dark!

PITOU: Indeed it is. Ready for a bit of supper now?

SARAH: No! The darkness must be resisted! Don't you understand—? *[brief searching pause; one hand drawn briefly across her eyes]* I have another idea!

PITOU: Oh, no.

SARAH: *[reviving]* You will be Mister Jarrett now! Yes, the terrible Mister William Edward Jarrett!

PITOU: But I know absolutely nothing about—

SARAH: Ssshh! It's evening, late evening! Near Boston! My private railway car has paused, to permit a herd of dairy cattle to cross the track.

PITOU: *[sits wearily]* Are you sure they aren't buffaloes?

SARAH: No! Near Boston? The terrible Mister Jarrett managed, or managed to mismanage, all my early American tours. A huge surly Britisher with mustachios and a foul eternal cigar! Of course you never met him, Pitou. He died, centuries ago, in Panama. Correction: he died, centuries ago, *of* Panama. But this particular evening, eighteen-eighty-something, having just managed to survive Boston, I am attempting to forget Mister Jarrett, and to rest! *[leans back and closes her eyes]* But suddenly here he is, the old bandit, snorting and pounding at the door of my private car, like an enraged buffalo!

> *[Pause. PITOU doesn't move. SARAH opens her eyes and glares at him.]*

Mary, Mother of God, is that Mister Jarrett, at this hour? Snorting and pounding at the door of my railway car? Near Boston?

> *[PITOU finally meets her angry insistent look. Then he resigns himself, sighs, and knocks on the table.]*

[closes her eyes] Who is it? Who's there?

PITOU: *[sighs again, stands]* It's I, Mademoiselle—Miss! Miss Bernhardt! *[Looks around vaguely, then picks up a pencil from the table and uses it as Jarrett's foul eternal cigar, his "character prop"; lowering and coarsening his voice, as William Jarrett]* Yes, it's I! Mister Jarrett! Mister William Edward Jarrett! *[clutches the pencil between surly teeth]*

SARAH: I have retired for the evening. Good night, Mister Jarrett!

PITOU: *[Jarrett]* Oh, no, Miss Bernhardt! There is something we must discuss!

SARAH: It can wait until morning. Good night, Mister Jarrett!

PITOU: *[Jarrett]* No, no, it cannot wait, Miss Bernhardt! Open this door! *[having wandered away from the table, now mimes knocking, and supplies the sound effect vocally]* Knock–knock–knock–knock–knock!

SARAH: Mister Jarrett, you are the one who concocted this hideous schedule! Parading me endlessly before the Americans like a two-headed calf! Even two-headed calves need their rest! Go away, Mister Jarrett!

PITOU: *[Jarrett]* Just as you say. Sweet dreams, Miss Bernhardt.

> *[Removes the pencil from his mouth and starts back towards his notes.]*

SARAH: Pitou!

PITOU: Madame?

SARAH: It is vital that Mister Jarrett speak with me! Tonight!

PITOU: You distinctly requested him to go away!

SARAH: The terrible William Jarrett didn't give a damn what anybody requested! He would bludgeon and bluster his way into my railway car, shrieking like a Cossack! "Bloody goddamned hell, Miss Bernhardt! What in bloody hell do you take me for? One of your goddamned cringing bloody actors? Or part of your goddamned hellish exotic menagerie?"

PITOU: But—oh, Madame, no, I couldn't possibly speak to you like that!

SARAH: But it's not you, Pitou! It's Mister Jarrett! "Bloody goddamned actresses, bloody goddamned Americans, bloody goddamned hotels!" That was his style, his unique charm!

PITOU: I understand that. I may even, to a certain extent, appreciate Mister Jarrett's charm. But it's quite another matter actually to speak—to say—*[trying it]* "Bloody god—" *[shudders]* I can't do it! Not even for you! It goes against every fibre of my being.

> *[SARAH emits a desperate sound, something between a sigh and a snarl, and covers her face with both hands.]*

*After a moment she lowers her hands again and looks
at* PITOU, *who is looking back at her, as inflexibly as
possible.]*

SARAH: Pitou. Forget Mister Jarrett's unique charm. Forget "bloody
goddamned hell." Simply say what you think Jarrett would say
under the given circumstances, omitting all obscenities. We'll
play the expurgated version!

[PITOU smiles weakly.]

Knock again, Mister Jarrett, knock again!

*[PITOU grins, clamps the pencil between his teeth
again, and knocks on the table.]*

[immediately] Come in, Mister Jarrett!

PITOU: *[as Jarrett again, mimes opening the door to her private railway
car and makes a swaggering entrance]* How did you know it was I,
Miss Bernhardt?

SARAH: *[gives him a withering look]* I am dead tired, Mister Jarrett.
What do you want?

PITOU: What do I want?...

SARAH: Is it about money?

*[PITOU doesn't really know. He looks at SARAH. She
prompts him with a slight shake of her head: "No."]*

PITOU: *[Jarrett]* No! Nothing whatever to do with money, Miss Bernhardt!

SARAH: It's not the animals again? Has my little Jasmine, my little
friend from the Congo, been nibbling at the upholstery in the
observation car again? Or at the observers?

Again PITOU *looks at her, uncertain. She shakes her head slightly.*

PITOU: *[Jarrett]* No, nothing to do with your animals!

SARAH: Well then? Speak your piece, Mister Jarrett, and evacuate my bedchamber! What in God's name do you want?

PITOU: *[struggles, partly as Jarrett]* Miss Bernhardt—surely you must know what I want?

SARAH: I haven't the faintest idea!

> *[*PITOU *takes the pencil from his mouth and looks at her, exhausted, desperate.]*

Unless—!

> *[*PITOU *perks up.]*

Unless you intend to trespass once again on my private life! Unless you have forced your way in here tonight, impelled by an Englishman's innate lack of sensitivity, to torture me again about my sister! Or about—about my husband? *[glares at him defiantly]*

PITOU: *[seizes on this prompt; as Jarrett]* Yes! That's it! About your—!

SARAH: You have persecuted my poor husband from the start of this tour! You didn't want to hire him in the first place! Now you want to take all his best roles away from him! And he is superb, he is brilliant in some of those parts! The best Armand Duval I've ever played to, certainly the most beautiful! Poor Jacques. I promised him he'd be happy in the theatre. What is it with you, Jarrett? You have something against Greeks?

PITOU: *[Jarrett]* Miss Bernhardt, I have coddled you through several American tours—

SARAH: Coddled me? Hounded me!

PITOU: *[Jarrett]* And, on each of them, you dragged along a different set of masculine luggage!

SARAH: Mister Jarrett!

PITOU: *[Jarrett]* Did I ever complain before? No! You never married your luggage before!

SARAH: Because I was not in love—I have never been in love before! I love Jacques! Surely even an Englishman can understand—!

PITOU: *[Jarrett]* I'm not discussing love, Miss Bernhardt! I am discussing business! The only reason any European would ever set foot in this Godforsaken wilderness! Your husband is a business risk! I won't discuss his shortcomings as a human being, I haven't got the time. The fact is, he's no actor. He can't remember his lines, he falls over the furniture. I don't know whether to blame his lack of training—or his fondness for certain stimulants! Exactly how long has he been dependent on chemicals?

SARAH: God! Who's been telling tales?

PITOU: *[Jarrett]* Take my advice and ship the poor devil back to France. Get him into a hospital where they can look after his sort.

SARAH: Jarrett! You are using a very lucrative position as my manager to launch an attack upon—Jacques is a fine man! Whatever his faults, he is at least a gentleman. But what would you know about that? A gentleman whose name I am proud to bear! In future you will address me as Madame Damala!

PITOU: *[Jarrett]* The American public pays to see Sarah Bernhardt, not Madame Damala! And certainly not Monsieur Damala!

SARAH: *[tremendously excited, a little confused]* Oh, Pitou, you are— inspired! You're even more insulting, more impossible than Jarrett himself!

PITOU: *[overlapping, as Jarrett]* Oh, no, Miss Bernhardt! You will stick to one topic at a time, for once in your life! One bloody goddamned topic at a time!

SARAH: Pitou—!

PITOU: *[Jarrett]* Your bloody goddamned Pitou can't help you now, Miss Sarah-Bloody-Bernhardt! I want some bloody goddamned straight answers, and I mean pretty bloody goddamned fast!

SARAH: I don't owe you any answers, Jarrett! Nor my heart nor my soul! Nor even my courtesy if you persist in—!

PITOU: *[relentless, as Jarrett]* To hell with your bloody goddamned courtesy! To hell with your bloody goddamned soul for that matter! Except for that slice of it, which you barter across the footlights for heaps of bloody goddamned American cash!

SARAH: *[stricken; completely caught up]* Mister Jarrett! You are forcing me to choose between you and my poor—and Monsieur Damala! I warn you! Others have tried that, to their everlasting regret! Jacques is my husband, my beloved! I don't care what you think, what any of you think! Jacques was and is and always will be—!

> *[Pause. Music. Through tears, SARAH looks out into the last densely coloured rays of sunlight. PITOU takes the pencil from between his teeth and watches her, nervously.]*

It was my sister.... It was Jeanne who introduced me to him. In Paris. Jacques Aristide Damala! But I fell in love with him afterward. In Saint Petersburg. At the Casino. He was winning, he was always winning in those days. He didn't yet need chemicals.

> *[She puts one hand cautiously on her lower right side and closes her eyes resolutely. PITOU sits at the table and scribbles with some difficulty in the failing light.]*

He taught Maurice to cheat at cards. But Maurice always hated him. I thought that was just the typical reaction to a new stepfather. *[pause]* Jacques did have the most perfect beard I have ever seen! All Greeks are beautiful at thirty. *[pause]* Someone told me, years later, that he and Jeanne had been—before I ever met him, that he and Jeanne were—that it was Jeanne he really loved. *[opens her eyes]* When we are young, it is their bodies. Their flat stomachs. Their large ankles, strong feet. The fur on their chests and their shoulders. Later—perhaps—we learn to appreciate the masculine mind. Such as it is. The masculine world: cigar smoke, honour, alcohol, and insolence. *[pause]* Later still, in our very last days, where I arrived, not without numerous mistakes—it is their bodies again. Eh, Maman? In our last days, where I have arrived without even wanting to—the old flesh sighs and unfolds and reaches out to grasp something—someone young! Jacques! *[pause]* Jacques?... *[pause]* Jacques?... *[closes her eyes slowly, deliberately again]*

PITOU: *[slowly stands and moves to her]* Madame?... *[touches her arm]* Madame?

SARAH: *[seizes his hand, without opening her eyes]* Jacques! There you are! Don't call me "Madame" now, Jacques. It makes me feel old. That's bad form for a lover, worse for a husband.

> *[She laughs. PITOU tries, gently, to pull away. She pulls him nearer.]*

Somebody once told me that Greeks are the best lovers. Except for Swedes. And who could ever take a Swede seriously? *[opens her eyes but doesn't look at him]* What are you thinking about? Jacques? Come closer. Very very close. Look at me, Jacques.

> *[PITOU looks at her, then away.]*

How old do you think I am? Go on, guess. I'll give you one hint: I never met Louis the Fourteenth. *[laughs]* Now guess, Jacques. Guess my age.

PITOU: Madame is seventy-five.

SARAH: *[laughs]* Jacques! Seriously!

PITOU: Madame is ... thirty?

SARAH: I am thirty-eight.

PITOU: Really?

SARAH: I know, I don't look it. I've always taken care of my skin. That's the one thing of any importance that my mother taught me. A woman must not burn herself to cinders in a few brief years. A woman must remain, must appear to remain unchanged. A woman must last and last and last. Kindness helps. You'll have to be kind to me, Jacques.

PITOU: We all try to be kind to you, Madame.

SARAH: Put your arm around me, Jacques. Now. *[pulls his arms around her]*

> *[Sudden noise, offstage: voices, laughter. Lights appear in the windows of the manor house.]*

Ssshh! What's that?

PITOU: It's Monsieur Maurice and the others.

SARAH: Oh, never mind Maurice, he's just a child. He'll learn to love you, Jacques. Give him time.

PITOU: *[trying to sound as much like himself as possible]* Shall we go inside now, Madame? See if they caught any?

SARAH: Caught any?

PITOU: Shrimp.

SARAH: Jacques, what are you talking about? *[laughs]* I never know anymore. Talk to me, Jacques. Tell me something sharp and solid. Tell me what you told me that first night. Our very first night together?

PITOU: *[disengages himself deftly but firmly]* Madame ...

SARAH: Jacques!

PITOU: No, Madame. No. It's Pitou.

> *[SARAH turns slowly and looks at him in the twilight. After a long moment, she makes a soft sound of enormous disappointment, and turns away again.]*

Madame, you know they'll be asking for you. Your granddaughter and her friends. They've planned fireworks. Fireworks and God knows what else, down on the beach. You wouldn't want to miss the fireworks? *[pause]* I think we should go inside now and—I think we should go inside.

SARAH: You. You go inside. Go on.

PITOU: And you'll—be all right?

SARAH: I am always all right. When I am alone.

> *[Pause. PITOU starts inside, taking the parasol and the album of records with him.]*

My parasol! You're not taking my parasol? Idiot. The sun. I'll turn speckled as an old lizard.

PITOU: The sun has gone down, Madame. It's quite dark.

SARAH: *[looks out into darkness]* Leave me my parasol. There's a merciless moon tonight.

> *[PITOU brings her the parasol, which she opens and*

holds above her head. Pause. He doesn't move.]

Pitou. You're not still here?

PITOU: No, Madame.

[He hurries off into the house. Pause.]

SARAH: I threw everything, all the pillows, off our bed. I wanted nothing, absolutely nothing, between us. His eyes were closed. "Are you really sleeping, Jacques?" "No." "What are you thinking about?" "Nothing." He put his arm around me. Across my breasts. "You ask too many questions, Madame Sarah. What is it you want? To crawl right inside me? To live inside my skin?" "I don't know, Jacques. Maybe. If that's what it means to love you, to live only for you!" *[pause]* And so I did! I lived only for you, loved only you, Jacques. Even in those very last days, long after the world at large had learned to despise you, had sickened of you! I still loved you! All through that endless unendurable afternoon, in that lightless airless room on the rue d'Antin. I sat with you, held you for the very last time. The bedclothes were filthy. And the floor was littered with thousands of little empty glass bottles. Drained of their morphine or opium or cocaine. And your body—which had been an object of worship for me, Jacques—your body, your arms and legs were defiled with thousands of needle scars! Some of them already swollen, infected! You leered at me from under bruised eyelids. And you grinned! "Well, what now, Madame Sarah? Do you still want to crawl inside—to live inside this skin?" And I still loved you, yes! Held you and told your stories. I told you all about my days in the convent. Mére Sainte Sophie and the grey sisters. Perfectly still at night on their hard grey beds. Waiting for Jesus and death. How I came to love that life, that lack of life. How I begged my mother to let me stay, to let me die there with my sisters in Christ. "Oh, I won't have long to wait, Maman! I will die very young, I'm sure of that. My pure young spirit will rise through the pure old air. Towards the perfect eternal light of the stars!" I didn't know then that they were dying, too! Burning themselves to cinders! Deceptive glittering old whores! *[lowers her parasol and looks up into the night sky]* I trusted—I believed that you, at least, were immortal.

[PITOU comes back in. SARAH raises her parasol.]

PITOU: Madame? They're all asking for you.

[Pause.]

SARAH: Yes. I know.

[Pause.]

PITOU: Monsieur Maurice made me promise I'd bring you in. Whether you want to or not.

[He moves to SARAH. She takes his arm and starts out with him, the parasol still extended above her head. Suddenly fireworks interrupt the night, several brilliant bursts of light and many colours, overhead. SARAH lowers the parasol, startled, frightened.]

SARAH: Dear God! What's that, Pitou? Not the sun again! Already?

[Darkness. Music.]

❋ ❋ ❋

[The terrace, many hours later. Moonlight.

A hurricane lamp flickers on a pedestal at one side. The gillyflowered blue folder of notes for the Memoir is on the wicker table, among other customary clutter.

Music. SARAH comes in slowly, in her white nightdress. Behind her she drags the open parasol, like a weary child. Under her other arm she clutches a large battered and discoloured make-up box. She moves about the terrace slowly, staring up at the stars.

After a moment PITOU comes in from the house, in his robe, trousers, and bedroom slippers. He watches SARAH uneasily for a moment. Then suddenly, inspired, he takes a pencil from the table, clamps it between his teeth, and speaks to her, coarse and surly.]

PITOU: *[Jarrett's voice]* Bloody goddamned hell, Miss Bernhardt! So this is what you call getting your bloody goddamned rest!

SARAH: *[turns and stares at him]* Pitou?...

PITOU: *[Jarrett]* Stalking about in the middle of the bloody goddamned night!

SARAH: Pitou, don't.

PITOU: *[Jarrett]* How in bloody goddamned hell you manage to remain as bloody goddamned attractive as you are is a bloody goddamned wonder to me!

SARAH: Stop!

[Pause. PITOU takes the pencil from his mouth, crestfallen.]

I forbid you to humour me! So blatantly. You and Maurice and the world at large! I am not some ancient child to be sent off to bed with a quick kiss and a promise: "We shall finish your little story tomorrow, Sarah." I am less of a child than the rest of you on this infantile planet. I know that tomorrow is an illusion! *[pause]* Pitou. I am going to die very soon.

PITOU: Impossible.

SARAH: Oh—you men! You eat and sleep and make love and drop dead without the least sense of occasion! But a woman has a more highly developed sense of timing. I am going to die very soon.

PITOU: You promised your granddaughter you'd live to be at least a hundred and three.

SARAH: *[drops the parasol and slumps into a chair, clinging to the make-up box]* You, more than anyone, should know I never keep promises! *[pause]* Pitou?...

PITOU: Yes, I know! *[moves to her]* Now you wish you'd stayed in your nice warm bed. Let me help you—

SARAH: *[pulls free]* No! I must understand, I must make sense of all this! *[gestures vaguely all around, at the notes, the sky, the sea]* Somehow!

PITOU: What've you got there? Your make-up box?

SARAH: Yes.

PITOU: Better give it to me. *[reaches for it]*

SARAH: *[slaps him away]* Hands off, it's mine! It's the one thing that is still mine. My box of disguises.

PITOU: You know it's nearly five o'clock in the morning?

SARAH: *[clutching the box]* This! My youth, my colour, my lips, and my eyes! This young skin I can still crawl inside!

PITOU: You're getting it all over your nightgown! *[reaches for the box again]*

SARAH: *[slaps at him again]* No! I need it! I can't allow myself to be seen like this! So old. Out of my disguise!

PITOU: To be seen? By whom?

SARAH: Her! *[gestures vaguely towards the sky]* That shimmering deceptive grinning dying old cocotte! The sun! Should she have the unmitigated audacity to come back out here and face me!

[She slams the make-up box down on the table, shoving notes, inkwells, etc., aside. She opens the box. PITOU starts towards the house.]

PITOU: I'm going to wake Monsieur Maurice.

SARAH: Leave Maurice alone! Idiot—! They didn't catch any shrimp yesterday, did they? Maurice and the doctor and whoever?

PITOU: Only a few small ones. You should remember, we served them to you at supper. You threw them on the floor.

SARAH: They didn't go to the right cove. They were afraid! I'm the only one who's not afraid to scamper down those rocks. You have to cling to the dirt and outcroppings with your teeth and nails like some old—oh, stop tapping your foot!

[PITOU stops.]

And stop sighing.

[PITOU is silent.]

And, above all, stop staring at me like that!

PITOU: Like what?

SARAH: *[staring at him]* Like—like—like George Bernard Shaw! Oh, yes, I knew which one he was! His pinched little face, I saw it staring up at me from the dress circle, when I had the unmitigated audacity to give them my Hamlet! No, not Ophelia, not Gertrude! Prince Hamlet himself! And in England! Oh, the abuse, the ordure they hurled at me from their prissy little newspapers! Especially that vile old Puritan, G.B. Shaw! God— *[stands rigid with fury]* God, I want to outlive that man! George Bernard Shaw is one person whose funeral I would forgo all other entertainments to attend!

[Pause. She wilts somewhat and looks out to sea. PITOU

[handwritten: She should have been able to do Hamlet despite her sex. No one judged her on her acting]

*wraps his robe more tightly about himself and sits,
huddled on a bench.]*

But none of them really understood. Not even in my own country, in my own language. Who in God's name did they think I
was doing it for? And what was I trying to show them? Didn't
they ever wonder? And, supposing I was not always so easy to
understand—and who is?—why couldn't they at least give me
the benefit of a doubt? That great and glorious and generous
doubt, without which there can be no theatre, no history, no
aspiration, no hope, no life! I invented myself entirely for them!
But no. They never really trusted me. And so, I could never really trust them. And, without trust, what we do in the theatre
makes no more sense than what we do in our lives. *[looks at
Pitou]* Trust! Surely you must writhe a bit at that word ... Pablo?

PITOU: *[looks up]* Pablo?

SARAH: Ha! Did you think I'd forgotten you? Tell me again, Pablo:
exactly where were you, and exactly what were you doing on
that terrible occasion?

PITOU: Pablo?

SARAH: You bloody goddamned oblivious Brazilian swine!

PITOU: Ah. *[nods wearily]* Pablo.

*[Now SARAH moves in on him, haranguing him as
though he were Pablo. PITOU does not react or attempt
to enter into this role.]*

SARAH: You have the unmitigated audacity to call yourself a stagehand? Or even a member of the human race? You had only one
responsibility, Pablo—one tiny little job! To place my big mattress beneath the canvas battlements of Castel Sant'Angelo.
Leaping to her death, the divinely desperate Floria Tosca was to
fall only eight feet, and into a Tiber stuffed with goosedown. But
I couldn't even trust you for that, could I, Pablo? So Senora Bern-

hardt fell eight feet, onto her right knee—on the hardwood floor! The curtain came down, and out front they cheered and hugged one another and stamped their expensive boots! The President of Brazil, the Baroness Rothschild, and the rest of that mindless crew: "Brava, la Tosca!" But behind the scenes, behind a crumbling peeling Sant'Angelo, a crumbling peeling old woman fell eight feet onto the hardwood floor! While a lazy Brazilian toad snored away on her big mattress in his smelly little corner! *How can she account for people who sleep during her greatest moments?*

[She seizes PITOU'S shoulder with one clawlike hand. He gasps softly and looks up at her. She suddenly smiles theatrically, turns, and executes a deep bow "out front."]

Oh, yes, I took my bows, all my bows, as usual that night. *[another graceful terribly humble bow or two, holding onto PITOU]* And afterwards we laughed, remember, Pablo? We laughed together, you and I, about the missing mattress! *[releases him; paces]* For ten years after that, I invented my laughter and took my bows and endlessly rehearsed and re-rehearsed every wretched brute of a stagehand, Brazilian or otherwise! And for ten endless years, the greatest doctors of the earth swarmed about—diagnosing, massaging, burning, freezing, plastering—and finally giving up all hope for my knee! *[catches her breath]* And now? *[turns to Pitou, who has not moved]* What's to be done now? *[sits beside him on the bench]* What's to be done now, Doctor?

PITOU: *[beyond resistance]* Doctor?

SARAH: *[relentless]* What's to be done now?

PITOU: Madame—

SARAH: I only want the truth, Doctor! I must make sense of all this. I am a rational creature, all evidence to the contrary. My leg will have to come off? Is that it?

[PITOU looks at her and tries to speak but cannot.]

Is that it? Doctor?

> *[Pause. PITOU doesn't look at her and doesn't assume any new voice or manner for the doctor.]*

PITOU: Yes.

SARAH: When?

PITOU: Well ...

SARAH: The sooner the better, I guess?

PITOU: Yes—Madame, I just can't—! *[looks at her]* Yes.

SARAH: You're afraid of infection? Infection, which must have already spread throughout most of—? So you'll have to take almost all my leg? Above the knee? Is that correct, Doctor?

> *[Pause. PITOU says nothing and cannot look at her. She suddenly seizes his hand.]*

Oh, God. God–Jesus–Mary–and–Joseph. What a ... what a thing. *[smiles]* Mère Sainte Sophie used to say I had a vulgar expression for every occasion, no matter how nasty. But I must confess, at this moment, to a sudden loss of vocabulary. I look at my life. At myself. At this—this!—which I can no longer—with the best will in the world—invent! And all I can think is—"What a *thing!*" *[releases his hand and stands]* Well, I must still make sense of it somehow! How will you do it, Doctor? Describe the process to me!

PITOU: Describe—?

SARAH: Amputation. *[moves to the table and sits near the make-up box]*

PITOU: Oh, Madame, please don't— *[changing his tactics]* A physician is not required to describe to his patient—

SARAH: Doctor, listen to me! I want to stare truth in the face. Now. This moment. I need that truth, however pitiful, however disgusting. To replace the farcical melodrama, the melodramatic farce of memory! *[fixes him with a look]*

[PITOU does not move.]

[more relentless than ever] Furthermore, I shall not close my eyes again—nor shall you!—until you have given me the entire vulgar truth, which I require!

PITOU: You shall not—?

SARAH: No!

PITOU: Nor shall—?

SARAH: Any of the rest of you! Exactly.

[Pause. They hold the look.]

PITOU: *[stands]* Well then ...

SARAH: Well then? Doctor?...

[She turns to the make-up box and begins to dab at the creams and paints, and then to apply them carefully to her face, using the flickering light of the hurricane lamp and a small mirror inside the lid of the box. At the same time, PITOU moves quickly to the table and searches briefly through the blue folder. He removes an official-looking document of several pages paper-clipped together. He looks at it and clears his throat.]

PITOU: *[reads]* "Report of Lieutenant-Colonel Denucé, surgeon, attached to the military hospital at Bordeaux. Fourteenth of February, nineteen-fifteen."

SARAH: Saint Valentine's Day! And now, the details of the operation, Doctor. Every single word.

PITOU: *[reads, with difficulty]* "Due to the hazards of gangrene, in Madame Bernhardt's case it was necessary to perform an 'open' or—or 'guillotine' amputation." *[clears his throat]*

SARAH: Go on, go on. My God, you're a surgeon. Your daily commerce is pain and loss. *[continues her make-up]*

PITOU: *[forces himself to read]* "We made the customary circular incision, seven and three-quarter inches above the right knee."
[Pause.]

SARAH: Continue.

PITOU: *[reads]* "We severed the skin and the subcutaneous tissue, and allowed them the customary forty-five seconds to retract. We then proceeded to incise the deep fascia and muscle in thin layers."

SARAH: Continue.

PITOU: *[reads]* "We cut the bone. Nerves and principal blood vessels were lig—lig—" *[clears his throat]*

SARAH: "Ligated." Continue!

PITOU: "We removed the abscessed portion of the limb, leaving a— a stump which—which—" *[suddenly hurls the surgical report down on the table]* Why in God's name am I doing this?

SARAH: *[not looking up from the mirror]* Because you were hired to help me.

PITOU: To help you! To help you suffer?

SARAH: *[pause; looks up and smiles at him]* To do whatever is required, Pitou. *[looks into the mirror again and quickly completes her make-up: lead-white mask, exaggerated crimson lips, eye sockets and brows darkened with kohl]* There now. Come close. Come very very close.

[*PITOU does not move. She looks up at him again.*]

Look at me. And tell me the entire vulgar truth. Don't I look—?

PITOU: Absolutely, Madame! As young as ever!

SARAH: You pitiful old liar.

PITOU: What do you want me to say?

SARAH: *[glances into the mirror]* Look! I just realized—I am the perfect image of—No, no! You tell me, Pitou! Whom do I look exactly like? *[looks at him and grins]*

PITOU: Your granddaughter.

SARAH: That drab little insect?

PITOU: Madame!

SARAH: Seriously, Pitou! Guess! Please? Time for a new game now, which we shall call "Guess Who, Pitou!" *[leans across the table, turns her face into the flickering light, and grins horribly]* Guess who, Pitou!

PITOU: *after staring at her for a moment* Is it—? I'm sorry, Madame, I just don't know.

SARAH: Don't be such a bad sport! You must know! I am the perfect replica of—what was his name? That miserable old stick of an actor who dreamed of reviving the classical pantomime! Oh, God, you know! He rented that pathetic old theatre on the Left Bank, just after the war, the first war, with Prussia! Remember?

PITOU: Madame, I wasn't born until after the first war with Prussia!

SARAH: *[stands, excited now, and paces about, more awkwardly than usual]* That poor hideous old stumbling imbecile—he wanted to breathe new life—to resurrect that subtlest and most sublime of French inventions, the pantomime! Mother of God, don't you recall that old vulture's name?

PITOU: *[sotto voice]* I don't recall my own! *[retreats to a dark corner and remains there, praying for invisibility]*

SARAH: And naturally he selected, for his première presentation, in that crumbling peeling old music hall, which smelled of the crypt—*Pierrot Returns from the Dead!* Remember now? *[no longer looking at, or even speaking to, Pitou; lost in the memory]* That shambling old cadaver—whose ghost I could be tonight!—made his grand entrance! *[mimes a shambling grand entrance]* The vacant eyes. The smudged and ragged cheeks. The harsh Semitic profile! All swathed in threadbare grimy white frills, like a shroud! *Pierrot Returns from the Dead!* Staring up from the dress circle, we could smell him even before we saw him. We laughed. We groaned. We splashed handkerchiefs with scent and clutched them to our faces! But he—Pierrot!—he just continued smiling at us, rapturously! As though we were cheering, hugging one another, stamping our expensive boots! He bowed to us, very deeply— *[bows very deeply]* almost igniting his filthy wig on the smoking footlights. So deeply, it was difficult for him to rise again. But rise he did! *Pierrot Returns from the Dead!* *[rises from the bow]* Yes! Pierrot recalls the air! *[mimes remembering how to breathe, recalling the air, always as the miserable old stick of an actor]* Yes! Pierrot recaptures the sunlight, the delicious warmth, without and within! *[mimes reaching out and upward towards a nonexistent light and warmth, then drawing it within herself]* Yes! Pierrot feels it once again—that tapping foot, impatient inside his breast—yes, he remembers what it is to love! *[mimes Pierrot's rediscovery of his heart, sensations of longing; suddenly freezes]* Yes! But then—Pierrot suddenly recalls—with absolute accuracy!—what it is like never to be loved in return! His daily commerce of pain and loss! In a cold black fury, he remembers: "They never loved me! They never understood, they never even gave me the benefit of a doubt! They stamped their expensive boots and spent their

money, but they never never loved me! No, not one of them!"
[as Pierrot, as the old stick of an actor, slumps onto a bench, clutches
her heart with one hand, her lower right side with the other] And so
he wants to die again—God, please!—to return among the dead.
To stop the crackling and grasping—to let go, to unfold, to come
apart—to become the mud and the darkness, no matter how
silently—once and for all! [slumps farther forward, then suddenly,
as herself, gestures sharply, angrily towards PITOU'S dark corner]
Write! Write it down, Pitou!

[PITOU hurries to the table, his notes, pencil, and paper.]

[sits up, looks up into the dark sky] Write it down! That I regret
everything! Write that down! That none of it was good! That
none of it was beautiful or sweet! None of it was meaningful!
Not one moment! It never was, never is—never can be! Not for
me, no, nor for anyone else!

[PITOU sits but does not write. He watches her,
exhausted, distraught.]

That is my little curtain speech—my ultimate encyclical to the
world at large! Write it down! That wheezing old whore, the sun,
is right to consume herself as quickly as she can! The stars are
right to welcome in the cold and the darkness! It is what we all
should do, and sooner rather than later, if we weren't all such
greedy hungry stupid children! [glances at PITOU] You're not writing this down?

PITOU: No, Madame.

SARAH: Why not?

PITOU: I knew this would happen! All day long—for days and days
now, I tried to warn you—!

SARAH: Write it down, Pitou!

PITOU: Madame—I refuse.

SARAH: *[stands and moves towards him, struggling]* You—! You may not refuse! You are not a thing that can refuse! You are merely that spineless soulless thing that I found on a beach at low tide and hired to help me!

> *[PITOU stands, facing her.]*

Sit down and write!

PITOU: *[all the fight that's left in him]* No! I don't believe you really want me to. It's not really you speaking. It's the wretched hour, it's—this climate! I don't believe you think or feel any of that. And I will not write it down!

> *[They are face-to-face across the little table.]*

SARAH: You will write.

PITOU: No.

> *[Pause.]*

SARAH: You—will—write!

PITOU: No!

> *[Pause.]*

SARAH: Then I will! *[moves around the table, shoving him aside]* I will do this, too! As I have always done everything! Alone! *[sits, leans very close to the table, and begins to scribble frantically]* I will tell the entire vulgar truth! And I will get the names and dates and places straight! And I will not file all of life's hideous disappointments under the single letter "P"!

PITOU: *[at the same time]* I've already written on that page! You don't even know—! What are you writing?

SARAH: The truth! That there is no sense, no purpose to it all! No reason for life, any more than there is for theatre! No sense in living or helping others to live, or even in writing— *[laughs wildly]* in writing it all down!

> *[PITOU watches her for an instant longer, then turns to go. SARAH immediately catches him with one clawlike hand.]*

Where do you think you're going?

PITOU: Inside! *[tries to pull free]*

SARAH: No! You will stay—and—!

PITOU: *[pulling]* And do what?

SARAH: *[stands, clinging to him]* You will stay, even in the mud and darkness, and—!

PITOU: And what?

SARAH: Witness!

> *[They struggle. PITOU fiercely pries her hands loose from his arms.]*

PITOU: *[retreating]* Madame—I'm frightened! I can't! *[rushes off, into the dark manor house.]*

SARAH: *[thunders]* Coward! *[pause; quieter, hoarsely]* Bloody—god-damned—!

> *[Pause. She remains standing, leaning against the table. After a moment she stares down at what she has scribbled on the used paper. She reaches out, grabs it, wads it up together with several other pages of notes. She hurls it away from her, into the darkness. Pause.]*

[whispers] Pitou?...

[She shudders. Then she gasps hoarsely and stabs one hand into her lower right side and the other into her bosom. She bites her lip hard, her face contorted. She tries to move away from the table, towards the house. After an agonizing step or two, she stops and gasps again, louder. She closes her eyes and sways for a moment, then grows very still. A long frozen silence. Then she exhales a long dry breath and crumples, falling full-length onto the terrace flagstones. Pause. The sea is heard, off, breaking against the rough beach. A first glimmer of dawn can be discerned beyond the manor house and the surrounding balustrade.

After a moment PITOU *comes back in with a bottle of pills and a carafe of water on a tray. He looks all around and discovers* SARAH *after a brief frantic search. Then he really panics. He drops the tray on a bench and dashes to* SARAH. *He kneels beside her.]*

PITOU: Madame—?

[He touches SARAH'S *face. She is cold. He feels for her pulse but cannot find one.]*

Madame! Madame Bernhardt, you mustn't—!

[Trembling, in a cold sweat, he releases SARAH'S *wrist at last and starts to get shakily to his feet.]*

SARAH: Pitou?...

*[*PITOU *freezes for an instant, then turns and stares at her.* SARAH *does not move and does not open her eyes. Pause.]*

Pitou?...

PITOU: *[catches his breath, almost a sob of relief, and falls to his knees beside her again]* Madame! *[takes both her hands in his and rubs them]* I'm so sorry! I'm so—stupid! I thought—just then, I almost thought you—

SARAH: *[slowly]* I think I know what you thought, Pitou. *[opens her eyes and smiles at him]*

> *[Unable to speak himself, PITOU helps SARAH slowly to her feet, anxiously but gently. He carefully guides her to a chair and helps her to sit. For a while, there is only their laboured breathing, the soft incoherent sounds of their struggle. Finally SARAH is seated and safe again. PITOU props her up with cushions, gently helps her to straighten her clothing.]*

Was I—gone for a long time, Pitou?

PITOU: Yes. No! I don't know! Oh, God, how could I have left you when—? And how could I ever have explained to Monsieur Maurice—? I am responsible for Madame, but I ran away like—like a bloody goddamned coward!

> *[SARAH takes his hand firmly in hers. PITOU looks at her.]*

SARAH: Nobody is responsible for me, Pitou. Not at my age. *[smiles]*

> *[PITOU tries to smile back at her. Gradually he stops shaking.]*

Shrimp live in mud

Besides—it was a wonderful thing! To plunge into the mud and darkness. And then, to be able to return. For a little while at least. I've never been so afraid, never in all my life. Yet it was completely, immensely wonderful! Do you understand? *[pause]* I'm a little cold now. Freeing experience. I'm still here and I still have power (make-up)

> *[PITOU looks around, then hurries to a bench and fetches a huge bulky brown fur. He hurries back to SARAH and covers her with the fur, tucking it in around her.]*

Ah, my gigantic fearsome beast. I shot him myself, you know.

PITOU: I know.

> *[It is growing lighter. SARAH looks all around at the debris strewn across the terrace, the abandoned parasol, the scattered notes and shreds of paper, the clutter around the make-up box, etc.]*

SARAH: I've made a hell of a mess.

PITOU: Yes.

SARAH: I'm sorry.

PITOU: Well, I should go inside now and fetch Doctor Marot. He'll want to have a look at you before—

SARAH: No. Doctors are all fools or worse. I'll have a small cognac instead.

PITOU: Cognac? At this hour?

SARAH: I no longer divide my life into hours, only into centuries. A cognac, not too small. If I sip it, it should last me all morning.

PITOU: Might I suggest a cordial instead? Or maybe a little sherry? With your pills?

SARAH: Cognac, Pitou!

PITOU: At once. *[goes to the refreshment trolley and pours a very small glass of brandy, then moves to the tray he brought in earlier and collects her pills]* There's nothing worse on this earth than cognac on an empty stomach. My mother wouldn't allow it in our house. She used to say to my father, "If you want to kill yourself, why don't you just drink arsenic?"

> *[He brings SARAH the cognac and a handful of pills.*

She tosses the latter aside and takes a sip of cognac.]

SARAH: Your mother was a fool, Pitou.

> *[It grows lighter.* PITOU *moves to the hurricane lamp and extinguishes it.]*

[resolutely, calmly] And now ... there is something I must say.

PITOU: Yes, Madame, I'm listening. Or shall I write—?

SARAH: No. There is only one other creature on God's earth who could understand completely what I must say at this moment. I want to speak with him.

PITOU: With him?

SARAH: Yes. *[takes another sip of cognac and fixes* PITOU *with a look]* Oscar Wilde.

PITOU: *[pause; realizes what she's asking]* Oh, no, Madame, please—

SARAH: Yesterday you were whining that I never let you portray men.

PITOU: But—I'd rather be a woman than Oscar Wilde!

SARAH: Oh, God, if he were here and heard you say so!

PITOU: Oscar Wilde is dead, Madame.

SARAH: Dead? Oscar Wilde? *[pause]* Maybe you're right. So, you're not only speaking ill of a poet but of the dead! Both mortal sins.

PITOU: Not as mortal as some Mister Wilde indulged in. Perhaps invented.

SARAH: Pitou!

PITOU: It was in all the newspapers.

SARAH: Oh, don't talk to me about newspapers! You know what they said about me? That my relations with my pet tiger verged on the unnatural! Poor old Suzy, as if she'd have been interested in anything of that sort! That I slept nude in a mahogany coffin and very rarely alone!

PITOU: But you told me that yourself.

SARAH: I never said "mahogany"! I'm an actress, I can't afford mahogany!

> *[PITOU starts to reply.]*

Quiet! *[pause]* The last time I ever saw Oscar Wilde—he was sitting on a deserted beach—memorizing the Mediterranean. A perfect place for us to speak quietly about the things that really matter. *[pushes the fur aside and stands]* I came up softly behind him. He was sitting in an enormous deck chair *[points out a seat to Pitou]* Sitting!

> *[PITOU sighs, then goes and sits where she points.]*

I must've been the last person on earth Oscar expected to see. He is staring at three young bathers as they dash through the spray.

PITOU: I'm sure at least two of them are boys.

SARAH: What difference does that make?

PITOU: To me, none. To Mister Wilde, considerable.

SARAH: No. Oscar is old and sick now. He's come to Saint-Tropez for the sun and to escape his creditors.

> *[PITOU looks at her dubiously. She directs his attention "forward," towards the imaginary bathers and spray. PITOU looks in that direction. SARAH reaches down and gracefully retrieves the parasol, which she lifts above her head. She comes up softly behind PITOU and taps him on the shoulder.]*

Hello, Oscar.

> *[PITOU turns and looks up at her, then smiles. He speaks, as Oscar Wilde, in a voice that is quiet, exhausted, gentle, very much like his own.]*

PITOU: *[Oscar Wilde]* My dear Sarah! Divine Sarah. Pardon me if I don't rise? You are the last person on earth I expected to see! *[kisses her hand]*

SARAH: *[smiles]* Well, you know, Oscar, I love taking the world by surprise.

PITOU: *[Oscar Wilde]* We've both done that, all our lives.

SARAH: True. *[sits nearby, shading them both with the parasol]*

PITOU: *[Oscar Wilde]* And now, I think we must not die, Sarah. Not ever! That would be the most breathtaking surprise of all. *[looks at her, terribly in earnest as much himself as Oscar]* Promise me you'll never stop, Madame Sarah—never leave us.

> *[Pause.]*

SARAH: I'll think it over.

> *[They both laugh softly.]*

Great God, Oscar, how long have you been sitting out here in this heat? Without even a parasol!

PITOU: *[Oscar Wilde]* I'm not sure. It seems forever. Where else can I go? My rooms are so empty nowadays. I've always had a terror of empty rooms. The conversation in the bar is odious. Especially when I am the topic. Yesterday I sought refuge in the kitchen. I watched a young man with a very sharp knife. He was preparing those little creatures, the ones they gather from the beach at low tide. For a soup, I believe.

She has an exoskeleton when she performs

What's up with the shrimp?

SARAH: Really? I adore those little creatures! *[takes his hand in one of hers, retaining the parasol in the other]*

PITOU: *[Oscar Wilde]* He tells me they have no nervous system at all. But the moment he touches them, or even comes near, they cry out in fear. Except—it didn't sound like they were crying—not to me. It was more like laughter. Small, private, but absolutely fearless laughter. God, I hope that I may laugh like that, when I see the knife approach!

SARAH: Was it dreadful for you, Oscar? In prison?

PITOU: *[Oscar Wilde]* Not so dreadful. Just boring. And probably very good for me. The plain cells, the plain food. The plain guards.

SARAH: I wept when they told me you were there. I wept for you.

PITOU: *[Oscar Wilde]* Truly? The Divine Sarah wept for me? Perhaps it was all worth it then.

SARAH: *[smiles; weeps a little]* Listen, Oscar. There is something I must say to you. Something only you could understand.

PITOU: *[Oscar Wilde]* I'm listening.

SARAH: The nineteenth century, Oscar!

PITOU: *[Oscar Wilde]* What about it?

SARAH: Do you believe the people who are yet to come—they're already here, in fact—the people of this new time—will they understand what we were like? All our joyous selfishness, joyous ignorance?

we strangle to create immortal art... that would all die out.

PITOU: *[Oscar Wilde]* Hard to say, my dear.

SARAH: But will they, at least, wonder what it was like? Torchlight. Candlelight. Privacy. Caviar, out of the fish and onto the table! Clothes, which did more than merely keep one warm! We are the last of our kind, Oscar Wilde. Victor Hugo is dead. And Napoleon, all the Napoleons. Byron, Garibaldi, Robert E. Lee—they are all dead! People in this new time—are very different. So busy, so terribly worried—so democratic. Desperate to find solutions that will pacify everyone, though they please no one. We weren't like that.

PITOU: *[Oscar Wilde]* God, no. We never sought to pacify. Perhaps that was a failing, Sarah, even a mortal sin. The world was scarcely a better place for our having lived in it.

SARAH: No, not better. But larger! Don't you think?

PITOU: *[Oscar Wilde]* Yes.

SARAH: More interesting, certainly more innocent! These new people—they know too many things. They have discovered that the sun is engaged in the agonizing process of burning herself to a cinder. And they can never forget that fact now! Do you think they can ever understand what it was like for us to live without so much terrible knowledge? To be so innocently alive that even Death could seem like a friend?... Will they read about us, Oscar? Will they remember?

PITOU: *[Oscar Wilde]* I don't know. They bloody well ought to!

SARAH: *[laughs]* So, you're writing a Memoir?

PITOU: *[Oscar Wilde]* Of course!

SARAH: Me, too. I'm well into my second volume, in fact. With the assistance of my secretary. Whom I do love.

> *[PITOU smiles.]*

A deplorable little billy goat of a man named Pitou.

> *[PITOU'S smile fades but not to a frown.]*

[stands] Goodbye, Oscar. Don't sit in the sun too long. My mother could've told you, it's bad for the skin.

PITOU: *[Oscar Wilde]* Oh, someone will surely come to take me home. When it's time to sleep at last.

[SARAH turns away and closes the parasol. Pause.]

SARAH: *[suddenly cries out]* Pitou—!

PITOU: *[doesn't turn, still half-absorbed by Oscar Wilde]* What, my dear?

SARAH: The sun is rising!

PITOU: *[as above]* Yes. It usually does.

SARAH: *[sniffs]* I can smell the sea again!

PITOU: *[as above]* Dead fish.

SARAH: This afternoon we will grab Maurice and the doctor and the others, and we'll all tramp down to the Apothecary's Grotto— what a delicious name! And I'll show all of you how to scamper down those rocks. Pitou? I believe I am getting my second wind!

PITOU: *[turns and stares at her, both horrified and pleased]* Truly?

SARAH: The sun has come back, after all! And poor smelly old Pierrot has returned from the dead!

PITOU: But this time, I hope, without regret?

SARAH: "Regret"? I'm not familiar with the word.

[PITOU smiles.]

It's August, Pitou. And a day in August lasts forever!

PITOU: *[looks away, infinitely wearily]* Yes, Madame, I know. *(It's been a long day)*

SARAH: *[sits at the table, closes the make-up box, takes a final thought-ful sip of cognac; suddenly very businesslike]* Pitou, in the bottom right-hand drawer of my escritoire you'll find the manuscript of a new play. A young poet sent it to me last winter. I put it away. I couldn't imagine I'd ever have time to do a proper job of it. Now I can.

      [PITOU stands, staring at her.]

Oh, it's a beautiful thing, Pitou! The opening lines are exquisite! *[leans forward, excited, setting the scene for him]* Fifteenth-century Spain. A very young Moorish girl—that's my part of course—has come down to the Guadalquivir, to bathe in the fierce heat of *shrimp* the day. She wades into the margin of the torrent, then sudden-ly stops and looks up! She speaks, to the sun or to herself, trem-bling: *[in a young exotically flavoured voice]* "They say in Heaven there is an herb, which heals all wounds, even those of love. But are the people of my dark race permitted to wander the roads of Heaven? I am so afraid!" *[turns and grins at Pitou; in her own voice]* Exquisite!

PITOU: *[moves to her]* I suppose so. But do you really think—to rush into a new project, at this hour of the morning—? In (our) condi-tion?

SARAH: What condition? Bring me that manuscript. Then you will take a letter to my young poet. I'm afraid he'll have to adjust the age of his leading character just a bit, if I'm to create the role.

PITOU: *[stares at her another moment, then sighs and turns to go; a step or two, and he turns back]* And the Memoir?

SARAH: The Memoir—can wait. We'll have centuries to spend on that. Later.

PITOU: *[stares a moment, then nods]* Centuries.

[He turns and starts out, pausing to collect the tray with the bottle of pills and the water carafe. SARAH is smiling up at the rapidly growing light.]

[turns back for a last-ditch attempt] But you know what poets are like, Madame! Especially the young ones. I doubt very much whether he'll be willing to make his Moorish girl any older, even for your sake.

SARAH: What are you talking about, Pitou? I want him to make her younger. *If she was criticized for Hamlet . . .*

> [She doesn't look at PITOU. He stares at her another long moment, then smiles, laughs to himself, as astonished by her as ever.]

PITOU: Of course.

> [He goes into the house. Pause. SARAH stands slowly, carefully, then moves forward without the least difficulty, very graceful, very young. She is a Moorish girl, wading into the margin of the Guadalquivir. Suddenly she stops and looks up into the brightening morning light.] *was a fist at the beginning*

SARAH: [to the sun or to herself, trembling; an even younger voice] "They say in Heaven there is an herb, which heals all wounds, even those of love. But are the people of my dark race permitted to wander the roads of Heaven? I am so afraid!"

> [Pause. Music. SARAH takes a step or two back and <u>drops the character of the Moorish girl</u>. Still very young, as herself, she smiles luminously up into the sunlight.]

[end]

[Handwritten margin notes: Still in pantomime Make-up]

Getting it Straight

How do you do this in our T.V. world. How do you stay sane in the midst of insanity.

SHARON POLLOCK

This world is a whole bunch of pieces which don't make sense.

Susan Wright [Eme] in the Factory Theatre Studio Café production, Toronto, Ontario, February, 1990. Photo by Nir Bareket, courtesy of Factory Theatre Studio Café.

Getting it Straight was first performed at the International Women's Festival, Winnipeg, Manitoba, July, 1989, with Sharon Pollock as Eme. Directed by Rick McNair. Set design by Linda Leon.

Experimental Drama - a collage
Sound bites linked through a
process of association

[*Light patterns reflect what may be bars, ribs, open
seating, the exterior structure of a grandstand, as seen
from the inside out. The patterns shift and change, perhaps as a result of the sun rolling round the Milky
Way, the earth swinging round the sun, the moon moving round the earth, or perhaps as an external manifes-
tation of the electrical impulses inside EME'S head. She
is hiding under the grandstand in an area used for stor-
ing incidentals and where a certain amount of garbage
has also accumulated.*]

EME: robin   robbin'   robinrobin robin
     spritely
     robin in the rain what a   nasty   fella robin
     pop song   *egg in King Lear*
     in the rain   digging   for your breakfast
     with your   long   strong
     beak
     somewhere
     someone is looking
     checking
     checking the ladies somewhere someone
     is
     beneath
     under here quiet here still
     now I say
     are there others?
     looking like
     others

no others
maybe others
bootsmell of, leather copper, smell of blood, salt
taste of tears, you smoke rag ends!
Shhhhhhhhh
I say, just to the ladies
they say, right back!
I say
fine I lied
calf's neck snapped back with rope small children
little
britches! one event only!
come on! come on yah come on gerry! chute 5 on
white devil! jerks and twists like a metal toy made
in taiwan that I find in my stocking and wind with a
key I say this is no kind of place to take someone
like me on a pass!
even I know that!
I have no hat
for one thing
I say just to the ladies then I go down go under
they sit
excepting for freida?
no
they sit
eyes focused on horse with eye bulged out strap
cinched tight rider's face pocked like the badlands
spasmodic like
myrna
they say too much medication not enough medication
myrna's eyes roll up showing
whites riding white devil!
then
I find my way under or
it finds me I say here is a secret here I think
here is a good place I think
of ubu roi of the nightmares of the blind of the nut-
cracker suite turned sour I think
of a very large collection of string puppets

hung
in a very small
room
backstage I think
of mime
and
panto-mime
and of
mirrors and of
wings
I think of the layman's guide to schizophrenia and of
ubu roi
again but I remember camus! I think
of
brown skin and tubercular chests and smallpox
blankets bought from the bay I say
how did you get here?
I think of giants and
of animals that speak and of people who remain
silent I think of cassandra turned inside out I think
of cat scans of the brain of satellite photographs of
the earth I think!
of real
and
unreal
shuffled
like a deck of cards play the hand I say!
they say
another sign
shadows
of a violent mind I see
white rain
garnet red the clouds I hear
the floating world it sighs
a little sigh they say I'm mad
I say enola gay little boy fat man!
little boy little boy fat man!!
Shhhhhhhh be quiet stupid
I think

[handwritten annotations: always prophesies doom / prophesies Trojan Horse / Troy / always prophecy / always prophecy life? / one that dropped the bomb named after MOM / names of bombs]

of
getting it straight I think
it began as a headache came on
just
after the news sweaty hands
pounding heart accompanied by
feelings of apprehension diagnosed as
a case of tension do you ever ride the bus watch
the news read the papers magazines books look at
people's faces! oohhhhhh lungs labour mind races
stop clock freeze frame cover story?!
they say
I'm mad I say
you know what I say
they say this
is paranoia this
constant growing fear of hostile forces that
threaten to destroy me advertently or
inadvertently covertly
or
overtly should death
dressed in a mushroom cloud or
strangely mute fall from the sky burrow in
they say
you can do it tinned food and bottled water will see
you through it, that and a good spermicidal jelly
they say I'm mad I say little boy little boy fat man
fat
i
isee
icey the woman the woman
I see the woman
who
washes
the floor in our ward cleans my toilet picks up the
pieces I rend and tear little pieces my hands won't
let go I!
see
a boat

that lies dead
in the water I see
it burning I see a small burning boat on the immense
blue ocean under a cloudless sky split!
split
by the tiny plume of black smoke which drifts
drifts from the burning boat I see it on the 28 inch
screen of a tv set with the sound turned off
help me I say!
I think of the earth like a bell the slightest
touch
sends tremors resonating round its surface the
woman
shows me
a small
photograph
of
a
family
on a saigon street they say
I dreamt it I say
getting it straight freida says
where would they get a camera?
this seems an odd question to me
maybe I dreamt it I
IIIIIII
iiiiiiiiiiiieye
I was always close to my father!
loving my father!
yes these are the kind of questions they ask you
here, are you close to your father?
yes
what do you call him?
daddy no not daddy father that's what I call him
father
they say his name?
they say his name?
I say r.d.
the initials you know that's

who is your who
— is they *world ward?*

him
r.d.
I say
his father died 2 months before he was born
they want to know these things so I
say my father was the youngest in a family of 13
yes the youngest child and the only boy yes 12
older sisters and him the only boy he
didn't
talk or say a word until he
was
almost 4   I say
maybe he had nothing he wanted to say
I say maybe he had a lot he wanted to say but no
one would let him say it!
I say r.d.
they say but
what is his name?
I say, when
I was little
my father took me aside and he told me
r.d.?
a mistake
had been made yes he
says his mother my gramma
you know
post-
pression she couldn't
fill
out the forms
well you can't take him home they said no one it
seemed worried about her depression it was her
fear of paper
concerned them but it's all right I say he says
he tells me when I am little
the nurse will fill out the forms
the nurse will fill out the forms
these things happen
his mother my gramma says

artie
not arthur but artie
she
was very particular about that, not arthur but artie
you can't call him that says the nurse!
why not says gramma
because
it's a
diminutive!
nickname!
nickkk! says the nurse
artie says gramma!
you can't call him that says the nurse! was the
nurse confused? gramma was depressed but even
depressed my father's mother was Formidable!
the nurse filled out the forms
but not artie no not artie at all
r.d. I say all a mistake right there on the form I say
my father confided in me me loving my father when
I was little
these are things believe me they want to know
I say he
has no idea how his mother found out what she felt
like why she never did change it no idea at all
life is like that
the nurse was confused
or malicious
my father never knew no never knew no never even
suspected his name wasn't artie till
labour day
labour!
day the following day to be
his first day   _ Labour Day
of school when someone
some person or
some group of persons
probably female
slipped a note under the door of his room
I say his mother and him?

they never discussed it I say
his 12 older sisters and him?
never discussed it
he lost the note
I say
do you think he could have dreamt it?
they say
nothing so
I
zip my lips
and I dream
I dreammmm
I lie on my back in a field full of yellow mustard at
midnight
I look deep into time for the nearest stars are tens
of thousands of years closer than the stars that are
distant and far
time
being space
being time
my room
is square 1 second by 1 second when I run
screaming rushing hit the wall pressing in small
7 seconds by 7 square measured walk drift
in a dream
sloow
space stretches
like vowels,   rooooooooooom
grooooooows I see
the milky way holding back the night so that
fragments of black are unable to fall crushing me
and the mustard and
a very small egg
that I hold in my hand it
could crush
you too
like an egg
they say—
I say

nothing
I whisper
I'm not certain if I dream it or   if it dreams me
they say
nothing useful
I think, they will check the forms for my father's
name
I laugh!
I say, my grandfather rides a camel across the gobi
with polo
he is a man loves travel he maps the water web
from the rockies west till the land runs out and
stranded he stands on a strip of sand his eyes set
on a golden ball sliiiding down the pacific he
is a travellin' man rides a rocket to the red star
is a man loves puttin' space between him and
where he last slept loves
looking out
into time my
grandfather
works for the railway sells tickets in a rust red
station house 4 seconds by 3 with a potbelly stove
and the smell of creosote filling the air
measure
the dimensions of my grandfather's life by
economic circumstance standing behind a wicket
selling tickets to other travellers he only travels
in dreams
when
he
retires they give
him
a pass, he is an old man then, I sit on his knee
this is they way the farmer goes this is the way
the gentleman goes this is the way the lady goes
boom! fall in a ditch!
he hides
his top plate in his hand then he smiles and I scream
and we

sells tickets and never travels, when he does he ends up in jail

child's game

laugh
inside
my grandfather's head a black hole blossoms in the
shape of a rose, he thinks of the gobi, the pacific,
and mars, he
boards the train in winnipeg for the sault but gets
taken off in
thunder bay he boards the train in winnipeg for
drumheller but gets taken off in swift current he
boards the train but
my father
always
calls ahead my father
visits my grandfather on sundays I
go along
for the ride I sit
in the parking lot with
the top
down
on the car I
look up
at the windows the faces of young men cross
hatched with wire look down I say
ollie ollie oxen all outs in free!
I say ollie ollie oxen all outs in free!
the black rose
blooms in my grandfather's head he escapes!
riding a swollen petal like a flying carpet leaving
an empty shell in the corner
of his cushioned room
I sit on his knee
and he hides his teeth
boom!   fall in a ditch!
Shhhhhhhh under is safe is it safe? Shhhhhhhhhh
listen
whoop
whoop
whoop of siren flashing eye push!
Freida falls

floats feet
together arms
outstretched mouth an empty ooohh and a look of
surprise in her eyes
this seems less real yet I have a small stain on my
skirt there
are things
I cannot bear to think about I see
enola gay on the nose of a plane written by a midwest
american hand wielding a russian sable brush!
enola gay?
a short woman
whose hair has gone quite grey
the colour of her eyes?
faded
washed out by some internal bleach enola
drives the pickup out to the field with lunch
scans the sky for rain, snaps a photo of a
prairie sunset, sends it to her pilot son in the
pacific is immortalized on the nose of a metallic
bird does
enola   see white rain garnet red the sky does
she hear the floating world sigh its little sigh?
enola?
enola you answer me!
hear me enola gay!
weather
means a lot to prairie people
claude   → Man who dropped the bomb
eatherley
flew lead plane he
only checked the weather – did not consider any
it was good   other implications of
he gave the sign   his actions
claude eatherly
being most sane
went insane
they say
I watch too many specials I

hear
the voices of students calling for their mothers and
at the base of a bridge inside a big cistern that has
been dug out I
see
a mother weeping
and
holding above her head
a naked baby
that is burned bright red all over its body and
another
mother
is crying
as
she gives her burnt breast to her baby and in the
cistern students stand with only their heads and
their hands above the water and they
clasp
their hands
together and they cry out
calling
for their
parents but
no parents come and every single person who passes
is wounded
all of them and
the
hair
of the people
is singed and frizzled and covered with dust
they don't appear to be human
they don't appear to be creatures of this world
I have children
where are they?
I have a stain on my skirt   *neg, pos or both?*
maybe
his sister has them
or my mother where are your children who has them?
returned in a green plastic garbage bag or walking

The Pas

north from the pas till the cold sets in? don't think
about that standing in a lineup for stamps it's hard
not to try telling people that they say
try a little rolfing jogging gestalt
try a little est and sex and tai chi   *all ways to be heard*
try a little acupuncture
meditation maybe try that
try alcohol
try politics and prayer try a sauna just relax   *effort to heal or effort to control*
organic food
sometimes that helps
try 2, 10 times a day the bottle's big and it's
refillable try an institution try a smaller room try
insulin
electric shock try
deprivation try   *no one succeeds*
alienation try   *try try try*
hallucination try
isolation they say! this is schizophrenia this
psychotic disorder characterized by delusions
withdrawal deterioration and violent violent
violent!
my children
have grown and my mother is old now so
she said
you do well in math, eme, excel
in
things mechanical like change the oil and washers
for the tap she called that mechanical she worried
I'd never catch a man
you'll sit at home you'll be alone
I caught a man!
I sat at home
I was alone
myrna
myrna's caught 3 men —   *Gets it straight by marrying men*
that's irresponsible myrna
myrna says for better or for worse
myrna never says for good

why don't you just shack up with them?
myrna says it would upset her mother
your mother's dead myrna!
myrna says she doesn't want to take the chance
myrna
shoots the pills up her sleeve like a card shark
later she will chew her tongue in a feeding frenzy
myrna says at home she has a dog that growls,
a fireplace that smokes and a cat that stays out
all night, so now she doesn't need a man
I laugh
she likes that
she whispers I'm seein' someone and he makes
in the neighbourhood of a million bucks a year
I say that's a nice neighbourhood
what'll you have?
well what've you got?
myrna drinks anything that pours but
most of it she spills on her shirt
the tv is suspended high in a corner of the ward
in a wire cage
we could play a game
but
all the parts are missing I see the disappeared I
hear the dispossessed I know we can read a
magazine you know the one with all the pictures
of the women
who have made it
to the top it's all the rage turn the page
glossy photos of their children
very clean
and smartly dressed smiling
spouses country
houses and a long shot
of
some art I lived in a house in the country I lived in
a house in the country my brother bubu and eme and
mummy and daddy and me lived in a house in the
country bubu

is
bubu is
42 when? what? now! 42!   my mother always calls
him bubu he likes it
she cuts his meat
he lets her games aren't that important eme
he lets her games aren't that important eme
let bubu win the game tonight he sleeps in the same
room he
slept in
when he was little he sleeps in
the top bunk he keeps
his papers
in the bottom bunk bubu bubu has 3 degrees and the
only way bubu could win a board game is by divine
intervention
games aren't that important let bubu
win the game tonight we lived
in a house
in the country I
see

   [sings]
shutters green shutters
yes shutters and shade
I see the shutters
and lacework of shade
green wooden shutters
darkening shade
my heart is aching green shutters and shade
emily emily emily emily emily emily em

   [speaks]
we picked

   [sings]
berries red berries
yes berries and bark
I smell the berries

warm sunlight and bark
brown bitter bark
my heart is breaking sweet berries and bark
emily emily emily emily emily emily em

　　　[speaks]
bubu and eme eme and bubu ollie ollie oxen all outs
in free run! run! ollie ollie oxen all outs in free!
bubu!
how do you get from there to here?
spring forward fall back　　have
a coffee?
cream?　　no cream have a sugar? no
sugar
nutrisweet?　　petroleum
product powdered in a brown jar with coffee? and
the radio on top of the frig hap hap happy jack
and his cock a doodle doo crew down at click
wishing you and yours a hap hap happy hostage
takin' in beirut bush threatens to nuke nicaragua
to teach iraq a lesson I've had it up to here says
bush hemorrhoidal relief for pennies it can be yours
with financial terms you can afford am I on the air?
right now I'm on the air?
they're in the air!
the word is out the back pack nuke is in
ideal for bridges dams and similar installations
with a slightly larger model in the works for cities
over 60 thousand easy transport in compact car or
truck yes truck pack tightly
in one container
two slugs plutonium with explosive
good ole country billy on your country billy station
with I'm pinin' in the fallout of your heart good
pickin' on mass murderer in moose jaw pleads
justifiable homicide on 22 counts of
do you think thermo underwear would help in a
nuclear winter or should you stay with wool and
other natural fibers? send 10

superpowers threaten war over grammatical error
in diplomatic dispatch today
the dow jones reports today
we have the means to erase iraq from the face of
the earth today
we turn baghdad into an inlet today
a child died today
they say forgive your enemies
today I forgive a few of my friends today they say
they want 2 megatons he gives them 2 they want 2
thousand they get 2 thousand it's just a job the
corporation's into everything today he says technician
misreads metric radioactive release today I want to
ask you
if you don't have a basement or a shelter would just
closing the window help? I open
I
open I open
his briefcase and I it's late at night and I
I am making
cookies?
for
something
yes, for something at school, career day at school
role
models are assembling in the elementary school gym
at 8:30 for 9:00 and my job is to assemble bake
and convey along with the children some appropriate
bars
booth bay bars
a creative extrapolation from mummy's nanaimo bars
I open
his briefcase I read
his papers I read
things that
disturb
me I burn
the bars I
shut

the briefcase I
assemble
more—
when he leaves in the morning he carries the
briefcase it hangs from his hand he looks
different
I
drive
the children to school along with some
squares
I say
what are you going to be when you grow up will
you grow up going to grow really up?
yes these are questions that begin to concern me
now I
watch the news look in books ask around exploring
their
options to see
what they can be when they grow up also so   they
can answer the question everyone asks after they
say you've grown you know the what do you want to
be one and I
find
an interesting thing did
you
ever hear of
hypatia?
she's a physicist
yes that's the one
mathematician astronomer philosopher and she is
beautiful and she never marries and her father's
name it
never said! and there is a man and it says his name
and his name is cyril and he hates her
physicist mathematician philosopher science and
love no! not that word other words freida
says
take it with water and
cyril and cyril and cyril and his friends and yes he

has friends and they seize hypatia and they throw
hypatia down and they have sharp shells abalone
shells and they skin her alive and they throw away
the work that she's down and she is forgotten and
in
time
cyril
is made
a saint I
think
they want to be cyril getting it straight this frightens
me I
say nothing
say nothing shhhhhh nothing at night
we lie together no not together we lie
on the bed and I
feel
myself
slipping
slipping into hypatia's flayed and discarded skin he
lies
on his back he stares
up
through the ceiling small
elliptical
pillars pale pillars of light emanate from his eyes he
tells me
he's sleeping
the briefcase sits in the corner it thrums a low
thrum if you listen it
cannot
be heard a low electrical hum inside the briefcase
papers are moving a slow light succession of
shifting like dry leaves in the night
on weekends I try to discuss things things that I've
read and things that I've heard and he tells me about
abaca
do you know what abaca is?
it's a philippine plant the fiber of which is used in

the making of hemp
babbitt do you know about babbitt?
he does
he feels good about babbitt
buy babbitt! it's going to go up! babbitt is going to
go up!
babbitt? an alloy of tin, lead, copper, and antimoney
he's got holdings in babbitt
how do you spell universal inc?
ooo that's an interview question u n i
communications! that's how you spell it, television
radio film cables threading the the oceans
satellites filling the skies demonology! you wouldn't
believe the market in demons and if there is no
market create one! cause that's the way that we do
things! ethane formica gadolinium and the habile-
ment industry! husbandry, we're into that too
animals food we've all got eat, fish! I don't care
for fish why don't I care? something about their
eyes, buy ironium! and judges! you never can tell
when you'll need one once I was in new zealand
inspecting a government site at night and a large
nocturnal parrot shit on my head I maintained
control of the situation by making an off the cuff
remark a play on words for I knew the name of
the parrot, kakapoo! that's what it's called!
I think on my feet and I love to read! I'm a patron
of the arts when I order a salad with nasturtium
seeds I pick them out I put em on the side of my
plate I'm afraid I'll choke on one and die I don't
see anything strange in that, you do?
afraid?
of capers?
no, love to caper but not in the city I live in the
price of oil will go up it's only a matter of time
you know I've always wanted a peke but I've always
bought a shepherd I don't feel any guilt about
that, do you know what raffia is? well don't buy
raffia stick with abaca! remember I told you that!

if I could get a decent instructor I know I could learn
to schuss, do you know the women's washroom?
well that's where my mother would take me until
I was nearly 6, for years I thought the uvula was
part of the female sex organ, it's not! it's that
fleshy thing that hangs down right in the back
of your throat, everyone has one, men and women!
government enterprises!
from wadis to wall street we cover the waterfront!
that lost by a vote but I don't grieve it's all part
of the game

games aren't that important let bubu win tonight

zymosis?
he says nothing about zymosis
abattoir?
weaponry?
he says nothing about these things
I stare deep into his eyes trying to see who I
married
I fear for the children
the briefcase thrums in the corner
run away get away run! just one step then another
lift knees tendons run ligaments and bones just go
no
slowly walk slowly don't run I say just to the
ladies' they say right back no one around slow
freida speaks from behind me
slow measured pivot on right leg hip rotating in
socket right arm in graceful gesture followed by
left
push
freida
with her empty O mouth drifts down settles gently
into the concrete arms outstretched feet together

it's safe here

maybe I dreamt it

I would believe that I dreamt it
except
for the stain on my skirt which is probably
something I've spilt which is probably
we!
have a house in the country
I
of course
have not seen it but my grandfather has described
it to me many times my grandfather
raised his family in that house and so
did his father and
my brother used to say he thought he could
remember it from when he was a child the house
has beautiful arched windows and
big purple flowers grow under the windows and
there is a yard and inside
the rooms are fairly big and my grandmother
would keep them very clean I have a dream
sometimes
I am walking down the street in my dream and I see
our house it is as beautiful as my grandfather says
it is, it is a little smaller than I expect but the
flowers are there
and the windows
and then
I see
a boy playing in the yard and in my dream
I call to him
boy!
I say to him
whose house is that? and the boy says it is his
house and
I say
it is not your house! do you understand boy!
it is not your house!
and in my dream

the boy starts to cry and I understand that he is
afraid
and I am afraid
and I know that something has gone very wrong
sometimes in my dream the flowers
are a deep dark purple they look
like the blotches of blood on the whitewashed wall
where
the soldiers lined the young men up and beat them
and shot them I hid but my brother was very brave
and my mother was brave too for she held the flag
up even though it was forbidden she didn't do it for
the flag she did it for my brother!
sometimes in my dream when
I cry out it is not your house it is not your house
boy! we are surrounded by people they
stare at us
the boy and me
and we implore them to help us our lips
move but
no sound comes out at
least
they do not seem to hear us
they look at us and our lips move but they hear
nothing they
hear
nothing they say
my dream is a dream all a dream my house is green
shutters and shade says freida in white sweet
berries and bark is that true?
think about it
get it straight
no no wherever there be roof tarp cardboard on
hot air vent tree stone sand leafgrey dirtdark
or shimmering that is our house believe and act
on that belief!
I am afraid for the children
where are they?
they

are
playing I send a cheque to foster parents plan and
they send information in geography living conditions
and climate along with a snapshot he deducts it
from the income tax we go to a show although it's
hard to get tickets the briefcase
stays home they sing and we clap

[sings]
he used to be a manly kinda man
in the locker room he'd always been a hit
he had push and punch and power
in committee they'd all cower
when he made a move to stand they'd quickly sit

he played a lotta poker in his time
he'll vote a tory ticket all his life
he likes tits and ass and whiskey pq 118
and he'd get a little frisky
when he went to those conventions sans the wife

[speaks]
sans means without   he got about   picked up
the odd french phrase and a little more
but that was before   now look at his hands
they're shakin'   just feel his pulse
it's racin'

[sings]
gone gone all of it's gone
his push and his punch and his power
now his masculine part don't work worth a fart
he's gotta stand tall but he can't fake it all
a woman has stolen his balls
    they can take a small rod
    it all sounds very odd

[speaks]
I try holding the world and this in my head at the

same time

> *[attempted song, more of a chant]*

did!
not!
appear to be creatures of this world!
deep!
dark!
purple like blotches of blood on the wall!
real!
sharp!
abalone shells for skinning alive!

> *[speaks]*

he
hears nothing
I
lie in bed
the briefcase
thrums   I hear the wings of insects out in the hall
he pretends to sleep the hottish bodies of the
children move between cool sheets
I do not get up!
this is the way it is getting it straight it goes like
this
a mighty volcano erupts! he bursts into the bar both
his guns blazing! he paces! like a lion on the central
plains of africa like a raging bull he wheels in the
ring and the hot spanish sun beats on his back like
a nuclear sub that cuts through the frigid waters of
the polar sea in the arctic night like a million
megaton bomb boom fall in the ditch!
it goes
like this
people
die
people die
of kidney failure at the general
a light winks out

a black stick child eyes lightly glazed and flies
around her mouth a light winks out brown-skinned
boy falls backward scarlett blossoms stitched
across his shirt a light winks out so
so people die
they say it's in our nature
these things happen
what if
a million hiroshima bombs light up the sky
a billion viruses consort in pink moist passages why
then
if there be gods they'll
sit
on jupiter with weenie sticks and toast marshmallows
and when the dying coal that once was earth winks
out they'll
trundle off to take their rest on
orion
like boy scouts retiring to their tent
and if
they whisper in the night as boy scouts tend to do
in tents before they sleep
an epitaph for earth will ripple out like those
concentric circles from little stones my father
tossed in pools too deep to fish for fear of what
he'd catch
earth's undulating epitaph
They Died like Men!

this does not satisfy

they say I have a great imagination they
say
what are you thinking?
I say I asked Him that!
I say I thought inside his head was a cornucopia
of rich and vivid images precise perceptive thought
I say what are you thinking?
I say have the courage to fear

I say the more boundless the deed the smaller the
hindrance
I say reality is surpassing imagination
I do not say I opened his briefcase
he says nothing
I say what are you thinking!
he says, nothing
I see he's right
inside his head they dropped the bomb it wasted all
the people but it kept the real estate
they say who dropped the bomb?
I say his parents
myrna says don't tell them that!
I say it's just a metaphor! what are you thinking!?

I
think
nothing
I
see
impressed in ash 4 million years ago a footprint in
moon dust on the dry sea of tranquility
a lunar print
they say
what are you thinking? I say how many steps is
that? I say one step! I say did it take 4 million
years to take that step or just a blink in time?
I say a blink! and I can travel faster further I've
done it anybody can but then I find it's always here
and now but that's not necessarily bad I say
they take away the national geographics and
the omni magazine
I don't care
it's all my fault says myrna myrna always lies
that's what I like about her it makes conversation so
easy
we skitter over the top of things like waterbugs
the television glows in its wire cage its voice
silenced by freida

ghosts dance across the surface of the screen
which is convex and rigid like the lens of myrna's
eyes she holds her hands over her ears so she can
hear
what's that? she says
it's a car
what's that? she says
it's a child
what's that? she says
it's a car bumper
what're they doin'? she says
they're tying the child to the car's bumper
your child?
no not my child my neighbour's child
what's that?
my neighbour's car with my child tied to its bumper
what's he sayin'?
instead of confusin' all you good people with a lot
a military and scientific jargon perhaps a simple
demonstration of the premise behind the policy of
nuclear deterrence would set your minds at ease
traffic accidents!
we all know about 'em don't we folks
now suppose you could deter you neighbour from
runnin' into you on the road by seizing his children
and tyin' them to the front bumper a your car
suppose everyone were to do likewise
it's clearly evident accidents would decrease
indeed the chances of a single child dyin' on a car
bumper would be slight
perhaps by a miracle no child would die
in any event we can predict with absolute certainty
that on balance more lives would be saved than lost
and that's what nuclear deterrence is all about, folks
so when you hear balance of power holds innocent
hostage I want you to think
road safety and children!
myrna and I stare at the opaque convex eye hung
high in the corner

it stares back
it says nothing
faint grey forms shift in an off-white world
silence
what's that says myrna
uniforms
what's that?
flags
what's that?
fists
marching feet
martial music
tanks and missiles on parade
warheads
feed the hungry
silos
seed the skies with death
state
state

    [sings]
our state may be prey to terror and tears
rivers of blood may flow
heavens may rain both fire and flame
return the same   rules of the game
for fatherland motherland homeland
we have the right to die
we love our land   we'll make a stand
nation is all
the state will not fall

    [less song, more frantic]
let women wail
power prevails
won't profits fall
make conference call
get credit line
meeting at nine
grabbing a cab

Sharon Pollock [Eme] at the International Women's Festival, Winnipeg, Manitoba. Photo by Bruce Hanks

catching a light

> *[growing garbled]*
corporate might
banking a sum
get to the top
ain't gonna stop ain't gonna stop aintgonnastop
ain'tgonna they
say
manic myrna says they say as she sits
by the desk on the floor with
her hands over her ears
in order to hear!
they say I say boom fall in a ditch!
I say ollie ollie oxen all outs in free
they say do you know why you're here?
I say
I'm waiting for someone to run home
last one home free frees the bunch
isn't that right? I say

[handwritten annotations:] Ring around the Rosie (about the plague) Fear of disaster

[handwritten annotation left margin:] hide & seek

[handwritten annotation bottom:] who will free her from the der of insanity

I look for freida this is a face I remember
freida says I'm not mad I have a chemical imbalance
I'm not mad I have a chemical imbalance
compared to what?
I do not speak of the briefcase I say
I am guilty this is something I accept
they say
guilty of what?
I say nothing
freida thinks she knows freida knows
nothing myrna
says freida
is flat like a
super thin george
jensen watch in
profile she almost disappears casts only a
sliver of a shadow myrna says check it out flat
and thin circle
round I
see freida flat and thin inside her gold
george jensen cookie head are gently whirling cogs
and wheels if you
could pry the face off all
is still and
flat
im–pen–etrable which
is
what surprised
me
so her drifting down like some snow angel?
no
but
her george jensen head settles
into concrete the
space age
sealant
ruptured on this watch face no wheels and cogs
spill out no
microscopic quartz rolls like a fairy penny from her

ear
no
that's what drew me to her
she wasn't what she seemed to be   myrna
myrna!
myrna isn't here
myrna may be here
myrna says
get it straight myrna says
they
have
push and punch and power myrna
says
he
likes tits and ass and whiskey
I say
when
he gets
out of the shower
his penis looks like a snail that's
lost its shell
myrna laughs
although it is a sad thing
I don't tell him that
what are you thinking?
I say nothing
he accepts that
he doesn't know that I lie
I tell him nothing
lying beside him in bed I understand
there are things he does not want to be told
I tell him everything!

he says he is sleeping
I blame him
once I have opened his briefcase he cannot
plead
innocence
he invites people over

we sit in the den
he talks about buns
everyone laughs
this is a joke I think
the house settles a
fingernail scratches on glass outside
the window a tall woman in a yellow sari holds in
one hand a black and white photograph of a child
her other hand is empty I
make coffee I
check
on the children I am
watchful
I am
not
mad
I am
getting it straight
I am
aware
of the briefcase
I
have
the courage to fear inside
the briefcase is a reality surpassing
imagination at
night it thrums awaiting
release I
look
to the past for guidance I say
little boy little boy fat man?
I say little boy little boy fat man?
myrna says
can you fold a thousand cranes?
paper cranes?
folded paper cranes cry
spare me fat man can
we fold a thousand paper cranes folded paper cranes
cry spare us fat man cry little boy little boy cry

little boy cry little boy littleboyenolagayfatman! I!
say!
I say!
I fear!
I cannot!
fold!
a thousand paper cranes I say! myrna says go back
to bed
I say
when sons and daughters die, their eyes closing on
rifle butt and boot, can they find home from there?
I say, when children die in dusty fields and streets,
is there no shadow cast across the painted blue that
shimmers from the swimming pool?
I say where are the children's graves? those whose
sin it was to be conceived of parents who once lived
where their parents lived?
myrna says
look
and
I
see
one of those towns on a river
a small little town on a river small little town train
running through and one of those squares in the
middle square little square in the middle a bite
in the air we walk
to the square my mother my brother and me
it is large and I look up I am small and looking up
old
men marching mothers' tears I am little looking up
wear a poppy hide the grief watch a general lay the
wreath place my hand against the stone
granite grey
mitten sticks
trace the letters carved in stone
here's to those
who lost their lives
and the finger

in mitten
rough woolen mitten
traces alphabet letters in stone I see old very old on
a delta by the sea many bridges over water and the
sky always blue
like a bowl
bebe cries mama laughs and the finger in mitten
rough woolen mitten traces alphabet letters in
stone gathering of people where paths cross yellow
skin and eyes we find strange they bleed weep when
children die lift their heads hope for something better
and the finger in mitten rough woolen mitten traces
alphabet letters in stone this does not satisfy!

faces press against the glass
the briefcase thrums
the children twist and turn their sheets uprooted
wrapt round them like a shroud
he lies on the bed his eyes gleam through
translucent lids I say myrna!
myrna isn't here
I say myrna?
listen to me myrna there

will be

no
more
alphabet letters in stone for

you and

I
will   will   will
spin
a   a
gossamer
net
of

of what
of women's hands and
and   rapunzel's hair and
that net
will encircle the globe and and
if a person stood
on on the far   left star of of
the utmost edge of of
cassiopeia's chair!
that net will
twinkle in the in the
inky cosmos like like fairy lights on a
on a christmas
tree and
what what what will it
spell?
myrna smiles
love myrna
myrna laughs
myrna moves her hips like a dog mounting my leg I
hit myrna! grab her hair! smash her face into the
floor! smash her face! smash! smash! smash!
smash!

[handwritten: look at Myrna]

[handwritten: Myrna copes by "sinking" to base animal level. Emie is saddened by women who collapse into themselves. Has a strong morality]

I weep
privileges are suspended
freida takes me for stitches

I
I sit
in the kitchen I notice the sides of the briefcase
are bulged slightly like the pod of some alien plant
inside the contents ready themselves for birth I
note
it is locked
he carries the key
he will open it and it thrums secure in the
knowledge
I fear for the children

I am watched by those at the window
he is no longer him
I assemble
ingredients and utensils my
hands
carry out their task but I
am dead I am
down
and out and
down and
out
a secret is revealed to me I think
my hands are empty and in my chest a black hole
sucks my heart away and then
I hear
a voice and
in my hand I see I hold the key of truth and
in my breath a crimson throbbing grows and
I look up
I see the blue
I see
we are living
inside an egg and I
I see that it's blue
and the egg opens up
and a bright light
like a thousand suns and if I can open my eyes
just a little open my mind just a little try to
listen a little
listen
listen

      [repeating what she hears]
the visible world   is no longer real
it's shattered   and turned into glass
a mirror   of ugliness   agony   shame
you know the way   you know the way to change
to change all of that the unseen world
is no longer a dream   it's   floating   just within

grasp a   shimmering radiant   heavenly   orb you
    know the way to   move yes move   towards
that
he shifts in the bed
I listen
I say
help me
I say
I know what's on your mind
because
I can read minds yes I see the words floating in the
air like paper darts ping ping and the words say
tell me ping
tell me
I want to believe I want to act but it's hard ping
it's an act of faith piiing
you've got to feel the blue piiiing
you've got to smell the light piiing
you've got to see the egg piiing
then our paper darts
will ride the electronic sea bounce round our island
universe   kiss the outer reaches of the milky way
and head for homes where others sit and watch
ping! listen ping! read our words hear our thoughts
ping!
the milky way I hear you say, now where's the blue
in that?
I'll tell you where
on the retina of each and every eye floats an image
of blue an oval of blue for we are living inside of
blue
inside of egg and it's blue
inside of egg that never contains inside of egg that
encloses and now I feel this shout and a paper dart
as big and luminous as a crescent moon impinges
upon my vision and that pale crescent shining shouts
now
black and white photos of children are pressed to
the windows I am watched

I open the drawer I would prefer some other way but
the house holds nothing useful for this I am
prepared
for this guilt I am not
prepared for the guilt of
doing
nothing
I walk up the stairs all sound ceases I have
.entered some space between seconds air sacs of
lungs hang in suspension the prophetic bedclothes of
the children exude a pale lemon light I feel
purpose and peace and direction
he lies on his bed on his back,
I study him for an eon of time between seconds of
time
I see no one I know.
I
drive down
his lids flutter like a butterfly kiss and they open
he stares up into my face
he knows me.

yes
I am guilty of that
they say of what?

I let the briefcase hang from my hand as I walk to
the water I sit on the shore I use the key I tear
the papers to pieces I chew and I swallow the
disemboweled briefcase sits open and empty beside
me
I wait

the g plons in the
briefcase are as
bad as the bomb

maybe I dreamt it
myrna says they say I dreamt it
I say no
no
I say strike out strike down I say this is a lesser
crime I am guilty of that I accept that I hope I

have killed him, to have known and done
nothing? that is the crime of that I am not guilty
not guilty of that!

This is the egg talkin' to all members a the female
sex whether you be operatin' in a corporate world
surrounded by the pressures of the 8 to 4 the 9 to
5 swing shift night shift day shift not fogettin'
those with ambition and drive who aspire to
executive positions slave to the 13 and one-half
hour day I'm talkin' to you!
I'm includin' this call for action all women who toil
in the home the field the factory on and offa the
street in and outa the jungle every race colour
and creed first second and third world under or
over on top or on bottom the egg is talkin' it's
talkin' to you!   *King Lear*
What're you gonna do?

I say
go to the ladies
go beneath
go under
you'll find others there
I do have this stain on my skirt
but myrna will answer twice on the bus while
you
and I
spin a gossamer net of women's hands and rapunzel's
hair and that net will encircle the globe and if a
person stood on the far left star of the utmost
edge of cassiopeia's chair that net would twinkle
in the inky cosmos like fairy lights on a christmas
tree—and what would it spell?

what would it spell?

what would it spell?

[end]

Hosanna

— a play about undressing

MICHEL TREMBLAY

Translation by John Van Burek and Bill Glassco

Richard Monette [Hosanna] and Richard Donat [Cuirette]

Hosanna was first performed in English at the Tarragon Theatre, Toronto, Ontario, May 15, 1974. Directed by Bill Glassco. Set design and costumes by John Ferguson. Lighting by Vladimir Svetlovsky.

Photo courtesy of Tarragon Theatre Archives, Archival Collections, University of Guelph.

Act One

[A "furnished bachelor," somewhere in Plaza Saint-Hubert. A single room comprising living room, bed-room, and an off-stage kitchenette. A sofa-bed, a coffee table, a small bookcase, a bedside table with an enormous urn-lamp, a portable record player, a portable television, a portable radio: in other words, everything that naturally encumbers "bachelor" apartments, which are only so called because no one is honest enough to call them "one-room expensive dumps." It is an atmosphere of sadness and solitude.

The only personal touches in this depressing set are: (1) on the coffee table an awful plaster imitation of "David," as deformed and grotesque as one could imagine, too big for the table, and always in the way of people in the apartment; (2) an "erotic" painting, the work of CUIRETTE, from the days when he had artistic aspirations, hung over the sofa-bed but unframed; (3) a vanity table, surmounted by a huge mirror, covered with innumerable pots of cream, lipstick, brushes, and bottles of all sizes and colours; and (4) an enormous bottle of eau de cologne. (It is important that throughout the play, the audience be able to smell HOSANNA's perfume; a cheap, heavy, disgusting perfume; a perfume so strong that it smells of stuffiness; a perfume that has

*imprisoned HOSANNA for years, and which leaves
rather sickening traces wherever she goes.)*

*Through the window, every five seconds, inexorably,
the neon sign from the "Pharmacie Beaubien" flashes
on and off.*

*The phosphorescent alarm clock dial reads three o'clock
(A.M.)*

*HOSANNA comes in very slowly, making no noise. She
stands in the dark for a very long time, without moving. We hear her breathing, as if she were drinking the
air of her apartment.*

*She can barely be seen in the flashing light of the neon
sign. She should give the appearance of a bundle of rags
that is somehow standing up.]*

HOSANNA: I knew I shouldn't have gone. I knew it.... I knew it....

*[She goes over to the urn-lamp and lights it. HOSANNA
is a transvestite dressed up as Elizabeth Taylor playing
Cleopatra but infinitely more cheap. A Cleopatra-of-
the-streets. Her dress is in wine-red lace, heavily deco-
rated in gold lace "in the style of the times." The wig is
"real hair." Her sandals come directly from Park
Avenue (Montreal), and the generous portions of jewels,
necklaces, chains, rings, pins, and the cobra hairpiece
that HOSANNA-CLEOPATRA is wearing, and the ser-
pents entwined around her arms, all come from any or
several of the 5 & 10 cent stores or the "jewellery"
shops that line la rue Sainte-Catherine between
Amherst and Saint-Laurent. But despite this grotesque
get-up, CLAUDE-HOSANNA-CLEOPATRA should not
appear "funny." She is a cheap transvestite, touching
and sad, exasperating in her self-exaltation.*

HOSANNA stands for some time next to the urn-lamp.

She looks in the mirror over the vanity table.]

I knew it. I knew it.... I should never have gone in there.

[She approaches the mirror and looks at herself, long and hard, from head to toe. She looks at herself as one transvestite looks at another. She starts trembling slightly.

She grabs the bottle of perfume, douses her hands with the stuff, vigorously rubs them together, then turns towards the sofa-bed.

There, sitting straight up, she begins to cry. With great difficulty at first, then more and more openly. She never puts her hands to her face, she doesn't budge, always sitting very straight, leaning forward ever so slightly.]

Stupid bitch! Cheap stupid bitch! Stupid, stupid bitch....

[She calms down, then goes back to the mirror.]

That's right, Hosanna. While you're at it, get your face all streaked. Three hours' work. Half a pound of sequins! You get one of those in your eyes, you'll have plenty to cry about. Three hours' work! You stupid bitch.

[Silence.]

A lifetime, a whole lifetime of preparation and look where it's got you. Congratulations! Congratulations on your terrific success!

[The roar of an old motorcycle is heard arriving outside the house.]

Your prince has come, Hosanna. Time to shed your crimson robes!

[She takes off her gloves and tries to unhook the dress but without success.]

Shit! I forgot there were hooks. I'm going to get stuck in this thing, I just know it.

[A burst of laughter is heard on the stairway. A door slams, and CUIRETTE, in all his splendour, makes his entrance. Of CUIRETTE one would be inclined to say that he is an "old stud." As for the stud, only the costume remains. He is a stud grown old and fat, his leather jacket, once tight and provocative, has been too small for a long time. His old jeans are bulging more with fat than muscles. But as a stud, CUIRETTE has retained his arrogance and easy self-assurance, all of which makes him rather ridiculous sometimes.]

His name means Leatherette
↑
– feminine
ending
– diminutive

CUIRETTE: "Hosanna, Hosanna, Hosanna, Ho! Hosanna, Hosanna, Hosanna, Ho!" Christ, what a laugh! I never laughed so hard in my life.

[He sees HOSANNA.]

Well, what do you know, she's back! The Queen of the Nile is already on her throne! Hey, your taxi driver must have been scared shitless, the way he was moving. I bet he just opened the door and dumped you out, like a bag of dirty laundry, eh? I tried to keep up with you, but he was moving so fast, and I was laughing so hard, I couldn't even steer. You know where I wound up? In the middle of Parc Lafontaine. It's not exactly on the way, but what could I do, eh, that's where the bike wanted to take me. Hey, Hosanna, it's been years since I was through there. And you know what those bastards have done? They've put lights up all over the place. It's lit up, bright as day, the whole park. Looks like shit.... Jesus Christ, it stinks in here! How many times I gotta tell you, the place smells like a two-bit whore house!

HOSANNA: You ... what do you know about whores?

CUIRETTE: Smells like a fuckin' perfume factory....

HOSANNA: I said what do you know about whores? Did you ever get close enough to smell one?

CUIRETTE: Big Pauline-de-Joliette smelled like that. I dumped her, remember? Never went near her again. She made me want to puke.

HOSANNA: Poor baby. She must have cried her eyes out for a whole thirty seconds. By the way, what was her real name? Wasn't it Paul?

CUIRETTE: They're everywhere, Hosanna, everywhere. There isn't one lousy corner that's not lit up. How can you get any action in a place like that, eh? Christ, they even put in a zoo for the kids!

HOSANNA: It's been there for fifteen years.

CUIRETTE: And a theatre too ... I drove right up to it on my bike ... all lit up, just like the rest. Lights everywhere. Jesus, you can't even get a decent blowjob anymore. Not a corner left in the park, Hosanna. I tell you, everything's changed. To get a good blowjob these days, you gotta find yourself a two-bit whore in a cheap perfume factory.

   [He laughs.]

HOSANNA: Okay, Cuirette, you've had a lot to drink tonight, and I think we'd better go to bed. When you can't even remember there's a zoo and a theatre in the Parc Lafontaine, it's time to go to bed. We can talk about your perfume in the morning. Right now your two-bit whore has had about all she can take.

CUIRETTE: Smells like somebody died in here.

   [He laughs.]

Hey, you know, when my Uncle Gratien kicked the bucket, the

funeral parlour stunk like this. I remember my Aunt Germaine climbing into the casket screaming, "Don't leave me, Gratien, don't leave me!"

HOSANNA: I know, I know, and the lid of the coffin fell on her head. You've only told me three hundred times. Three hundred times you've told me that story.

CUIRETTE: You don't think it's funny? Pow! Right on the head. And then you know what she says? "Oh, yes, dear, yes, if you want me to follow you, I will. I'm coming with you, Gratien, I'm coming!" Christ, that was funny! And your room, Hosanna, reminds me of my Uncle Gratien's funeral and my Aunt Germaine. That's why I'm talking about it.

[handwritten: Perfume reminds him of this event]

HOSANNA: It's also because you've got nothing else to say....

CUIRETTE: I said to myself: "Cuirette, my friend, they've built a theatre on the very spot you made your debut...." That's not bad, eh?... Not bad at all....

HOSANNA: Yeah, and one day they're going to tear down the Bijou Theatre, which is where you're going to end up, and they're going to build a park in its place ... a nice big park with lots and lots of toilets ... le Parc Raymond-Cuirette!

CUIRETTE: Goddamn lights, they're everywhere. They've ruined it, Hosanna, they've ruined my beautiful park. I started busting streetlights, but then I stopped 'cause they were the old ones, and the old ones look kinda nice. You can't bust the new ones, they're too high. It looks like a baseball field, for Chrissake!

HOSANNA: Too bad it wasn't that bright when I met you, eh?

CUIRETTE: Hey, did you check out the taxi driver? Whose type was he, yours or mine?

HOSANNA: Fat chance he'd be yours, Cuirette. Taxi drivers dressed as women aren't that easy to come by. Even on Halloween.

CUIRETTE: Some of them are women....

HOSANNA: Real ones, yes, I know, stupid! It's not the first time in my life I've taken a taxi.

CUIRETTE: Yeah, but never that fast. Man, I've never seen you in such a flap.

HOSANNA: I wasn't in a flap.

CUIRETTE: You want to bet?

HOSANNA: I wasn't in a flap, stupid!

CUIRETTE: Sure, you kept your dignity till you got to the door. But as soon as they couldn't see you anymore, you tore down those stairs like a bat out of hell. And this time you weren't too choosy about whose taxi you got into, eh? You didn't stand there wiggling your ass and giving them the eye, did you? No, you grabbed the first one that came along, and you jumped in before the poor bastard knew what hit him. All he saw was a flash of red rags and scrap metal falling into his back seat, and someone screaming, "Get me out of here, get me out of here. I'll tell you where I'm going in a minute."

> *[HOSANNA goes up to CUIRETTE and turns her back to him.]*

HOSANNA: Will you unhook my dress?

CUIRETTE: If it takes as long to get out of it as it did to get in, you may as well leave it on till next Halloween.

HOSANNA: Listen, smarty-pants, if you don't want to do it, just say so, and I'll do it myself.... I can do it myself, you know, if you don't want to help me.

CUIRETTE: No, no, I'll do it....

[The phone rings. CUIRETTE grabs it before undoing even one hook.]

Hello?...

[Disappointed.]

... Oh.... Yeah....

[to HOSANNA]

... It's for you....

HOSANNA: At this hour? Who is it?

CUIRETTE: I don't know.... I don't recognize her voice....

HOSANNA: It's a woman?

CUIRETTE: I doubt it, but whoever she is, I don't know her.

[He starts laughing.]

Well, here, see for yourself.

[HOSANNA takes the receiver.]

HOSANNA: ... Hello....

[She stands fixed for a moment, then slams down the receiver and throws the phone on the floor.]

CUIRETTE: So, did you know her?

HOSANNA: Fat bitch!

CUIRETTE: Listen, baby, I've already told you. I'm not one of the girls.

HOSANNA: I wasn't talking to you.... You're not so important that I talk to you all the time. You're not that important! Besides, in that idiot outfit you look so little like a man, if anyone heard me calling you a bitch they'd take you for a lesbian!

CUIRETTE: Yeah. Well, I'm no lesbian, and I can prove it.

HOSANNA: You? You couldn't prove a goddamn thing. You don't got what it takes.

CUIRETTE: You want the proof, Hosanna?

HOSANNA: No thanks. I've swallowed enough for one night!

CUIRETTE: You're too much, you know that? Swallowed enough for one night. You really know how to dish it out, don't you? I'll bet your customers lap it right up when you talk like that.

HOSANNA: Oh, sure, I'm the funniest hairdresser in town....

[HOSANNA picks up the telephone, hesitates before putting it in place, then does so.]

And I'm very, very popular with the Jewish ladies because I don't singe their hair.... Funny and clever! The secret of my success.

CUIRETTE: Does my Queen-of-the-Nile hairdresser still want to get unhooked?

[The telephone rings again, and HOSANNA grabs it right away.]

HOSANNA: Go shit yourself, Sandra! Go shit yourself, you dried up cunt!

[She hangs up.]

CUIRETTE: You were hoping she'd phone back, weren't you?

HOSANNA: And you recognized her voice, didn't you?

CUIRETTE: No. Anyway, I don't think it was her. She probably got somebody else to do it.

HOSANNA: You knew goddamn well she was gonna phone. Another one of your stupid jokes!

CUIRETTE: No....

HOSANNA: Yes! Every chance you get, you ...

   [The phone rings.]

   Goddamn it, what's she calling for? What the hell does she want? Is she going to keep calling all night?

   [CUIRETTE answers the phone.]

CUIRETTE: Hello, Sandra? Is that you, Sandra? Hello! Okay, that's enough. It was funny the first time, but ...

   [A moment, then CUIRETTE starts to laugh.]

   Yeah, sure, but listen, put yourself in her place....

HOSANNA: Don't worry, she's been trying to do that for four years, the bitch!

CUIRETTE: Alright, Sandra, the party's over.... It was lots of fun, but leave Hosanna alone now, okay?

HOSANNA: Oh, so you're siding with me now? That really takes the cake!

CUIRETTE: Naw, I don't feel like it.... I'm going to stay here.

HOSANNA: You're goddamn right you're going to stay here....

[She grabs the phone away from CUIRETTE.]

Hello, Sandra, how are you, dear? I'm fine, thank you, but listen, it's three-thirty, and I have to go to work tomorrow, so if you don't mind I'd like to go to bed, okay? It's nice of you to invite Cuirette to spend the night, but Cuirette is my husband, and he's going to stay here. And Sandra, you've been chasing him a long time, and all the time he's been laughing in your face, so it's time you realized he's not the least bit interested in you. In fact you give us both the shits! Oh, you were very funny tonight, and you were very pleased that everyone laughed at your stupid jokes, but too bad you didn't notice how they laughed even harder every time you turned your back, eh, because your dress was so tight you split a seam, and one of your magnificent rolls of fat was sticking out like a big pink sausage. And what's more, Sandra, there's nothing so ugly in this world as a real yellow dress on a dyed blond!

[She hangs up.]

CUIRETTE: What a mouth!

HOSANNA: I must remember that the next time I use it on you, Rosa ... excuse me! Rosario!

CUIRETTE: Water off a duck's back, baby....

HOSANNA: Yes, but it's a long time since you lost your feathers, ducky. And if there's anyone who's not waterproof, it's you! Come on, unhook me, and let's go to bed.

CUIRETTE: I don't feel like it....

[HOSANNA stares at CUIRETTE for a long moment.]

HOSANNA: You don't feel like what ... unhooking me or going to bed?

CUIRETTE: You've been crying, eh?

[HOSANNA suddenly starts fighting with her dress.]

HOSANNA: I've been known to do that, yes.

CUIRETTE: I hadn't noticed.... I'm sorry.

[He goes to help her.]

HOSANNA: What do you want, five bucks?

CUIRETTE: I've had better offers.

[As if nothing happened.]

You ought to just tear it off anyway. I doubt if you'll be wearing it again for a while.

[HOSANNA stops struggling.]

HOSANNA: You're right, I won't be wearing it for a while. I won't be wearing it for a long time! But it took me three weeks to make it, and I'm going to keep it.

CUIRETTE: Sure, hang it in the closet, and every time you open the door, you can think of tonight and get real sad. Man, you just love to suffer, don't you, you really love to suffer.

[HOSANNA doesn't answer but starts fighting with her dress again.]

HOSANNA: That's one....

CUIRETTE: There's only one hundred and seventy-nine left.... I'm gonna open the window. I just walked by the operating table. If I don't get some air, I'm gonna pass out.

HOSANNA: Cuirette, please! Open the window, open the door, open the bed, open whatever you want, but for Chrissake, shut your mouth, you're driving me nuts!

CUIRETTE: You want me to go to Sandra's party? My bike's just outside the door....

HOSANNA: Go right ahead! And while you're at it, take a ride through the park. You can stop and have a good cry over the scene of your debut, which by the way nobody gives a shit about, even though you love to bore us all to tears with it.... Shit! I've broken a nail. That's the second one tonight! Shit!

CUIRETTE: *[opening the window]* I doubt if Cleopatra talked like that....

HOSANNA: Cleopatra didn't have to undo her own hooks!

CUIRETTE: Cleopatra didn't have hooks!

> *[CUIRETTE leans on the windowsill while HOSANNA continues her dance.]*

HOSANNA: If I can just get the first few, the rest will be easy.... Jesus, I hate it when I break a nail. It makes my fingers look all naked.... Can't do a goddamn thing with it.... Gets caught on everything too....

CUIRETTE: Cat's are like that....

HOSANNA: What?

CUIRETTE: Cats. You know, if you cut a cat's claws ...

HOSANNA: Oh, I guess I'd better file it. If I don't it'll just break more....

CUIRETTE: If you cut their claws, they don't know what to do....

HOSANNA: Hey, Cuirette, did you take my nail file?

CUIRETTE: It's sort of like they're lost.... They look around ... their eyes big like saucers.... Can't feel a thing.

HOSANNA: Cuirette, for Chrissake, it's not their claws that do that, it's their whiskers! That happens when you cut their whiskers.

> *[HOSANNA has found her nail file and starts filing her broken nail.*
>
> *Long silence.*
>
> *CUIRETTE looks down the street.]*

There, that's much better. Goddamn hooks, they always come undone during a smart social evening, and you sit there like a stunned duck trying to look beautiful while everyone laughs at you. But then as soon as you want to undo them ...

> *[She struggles with the dress.]*

... As soon as you want to undo them, they won't budge.... They're like padlocks.... I knew I should have bought snaps!

CUIRETTE: *[looking outside]* One of these days, I'm gonna smash that fucker....

HOSANNA: Who?

CUIRETTE: Relax, I wasn't talking to you.... You're not so important that I talk to you *all* the time.... The sign ... The Pharmacie Beaubien sign ... One of these days I'm gonna smash it. Between that sign and your perfume, this place is the shits!

HOSANNA: And me? Aren't you forgetting me?

CUIRETTE: You? You're as bad as the dump you live in. You stink of perfume three blocks away, and most of the time you're lit up like that goddamn sign. You oughta know by now, you make me sick....

HOSANNA: Yes, I know, and I know what you think of the sign and the perfume.... Whew, I've got to stop.... I'm all out of breath....

If I don't sit down for a minute I'm going to have mass hysteria.... Give me a cigarette. Hey, Cuirette, I'm talking to you! Give me a cigarette!

[CUIRETTE gives HOSANNA a cigarette, and she places it in a long cigarette holder. CUIRETTE lights it for her.]

CUIRETTE: After your cigarette, you want me to help you with your dress?

HOSANNA: No way, Sonny. I've always done everything by myself.

CUIRETTE: Everything?

HOSANNA: Oh, you're so subtle! Besides, I'm not going to let a few hooks get me down.

[Woman of the world.]

That must look pretty chic, eh, a woman with her dress half undone, drawing voluptuously on a cigarette holder?...

CUIRETTE: Not a woman who's been working on her hooks for half an hour and sweating like a pig....

HOSANNA: I'm talking about the overall effect, dummy! It's not necessary to go into details. Nor do you have to know what happened before, or what's going to happen after ... just the overall effect.... Regardes....

[She smokes voluptuously.]

CUIRETTE: Well, baby, the effect you have on me ...

HOSANNA: Oh, go take a shit!

CUIRETTE: That's how you take care of everything, eh? Tell people to go take a shit.

HOSANNA: Precisely. It's less complicated. That way you know where they are, and they don't bother you.... Oh, no, tonight I'm just not up to it. The voluptuous, provocative poses will have to wait.... Hey, wouldn't it be funny if my hooks got stuck in the sofa, and I couldn't get up! "Hosanna is dead, pinned to her sofa like a rare and precious butterfly."

CUIRETTE: See, you're in a better mood already!

HOSANNA: Like hell. If your hooks got stuck, you might develop a sense of humour too. It's called "trying to forget." Or is that too subtle for you?

CUIRETTE: So, are we gonna have a second round or aren't we? "Ladies and Gentlemen, presenting 'Hosanna-of-the-Hooks,' a new and exotic number executed by—and when I say 'executed,' Ladies and Gentlemen, I mean 'executed'—by the tantalizing, the seductive, the show-stopping one-and-only Hosanna, Hosanna, Hosanna, Ho!"

> [*HOSANNA lunges at CUIRETTE and puts out her cigarette on his forehead.*]

Hey, you fucking maniac!

HOSANNA: Don't you ever say that again, Cuirette, you hear me? Never! I've put up with a lot for a long time, but I never want to hear you say that again as long as you live! Can't you see I'm trying not to think about it? Not another word about tonight, not another word!

> [*CUIRETTE runs to the kitchen and opens the refrigerator. He takes out the butter and rubs some on his forehead.*]

That's right, do like Mommy said. When we get a little burn we put some butter on it, and the hurt goes away all by itself....

CUIRETTE: Crazy bitch! You could have put my eye out.

HOSANNA: Noway Jose. I knew where I was aiming. It's bad enough having a husband who's fat, I don't want him half blind as well.

[CUIRETTE grabs HOSANNA by the arm.]

CUIRETTE: It's a beating you want, eh? That's what you're looking for.

HOSANNA: Don't touch me! Take your hands off me!

CUIRETTE: Well, I'm not going to give you one. Why should I touch you anyway? You like it too much when I touch you. Eh?

HOSANNA: *[rubbing her arm]* Didn't even hurt me.

CUIRETTE: Oh, yeah? Try reaching your stupid hooks.... Go on, try it. See if I didn't hurt you.

[HOSANNA tries to reach her hooks.] look for images of being hooked

HOSANNA. Ow! Jesus!

CUIRETTE: Remember the other day? You said I don't have a strong grip anymore?

HOSANNA: You've got a strong grip for breaking people's arms.... But that's all.

CUIRETTE: Not according to Sandra....

HOSANNA: Sandra doesn't know what she's talking about, the jealous bitch. All she's done for four years is drool over you. And I don't know why, eh, because there's not much to get excited about. But then maybe two fatsos together ...

CUIRETTE: What makes you think she doesn't know what she's talking about? Eh?

HOSANNA: Don't give me any of your fantasies, Cuirette. I don't buy them. You've never been to bed with Sandra, and you never will. All you can do is make an ass of yourself whenever she's around.

[*Suddenly changing her tone.*]

She'd love to, she'd just love to, but not you.

CUIRETTE: How do you know?

HOSANNA: I'd rather not talk about it, I might get nasty.... Aw, come on, this has gone on long enough. I'm sick of having this thing on my back.... Just undo two or three, and I'll do the rest....

[*HOSANNA turns her back to CUIRETTE, who looks at her for a moment. Slowly he begins to undo her dress.*]

CUIRETTE: You could have put my eye out.

HOSANNA: I *should* have put your eye out. Nuance.

[handwritten: butterfly hooker (slang in Quebec)]

CUIRETTE: Okay, butterfly, you can climb out of your cocoon now.... Come on, spread your wings, the night air awaits you....

[*HOSANNA removes her dress. She is wearing panties and a bra.*

[handwritten: Are the dress & name coming off]

Silence.]

HOSANNA: Did I really hurt you? Let me see.... Bah, it's not so bad.... All you can see is butter....

CUIRETTE: Claude....

[*HOSANNA turns away brusquely.*]

HOSANNA: My name is Hosanna.

[CUIRETTE goes back to the window.

HOSANNA speaks to the mirror.]

I should have started with the wig. If I'd started with that it would have made more sense ... but I don't feel like it.... I don't feel like taking it off....

CUIRETTE: *[out the window]* It's true.... I am getting fat....

HOSANNA: What?

CUIRETTE: I said one of these days I'm gonna smash that fucking sign....

[Silence.]

HOSANNA: I think I'll go to bed with my make-up on, Cuirette.... I'm afraid of what's underneath....

CUIRETTE: What?

HOSANNA: I said I ought to change my perfume.

CUIRETTE: *[turning towards HOSANNA]* Are you kidding?

HOSANNA: Another perfume wouldn't make any difference, Cuirette. You'd still choke on it.

CUIRETTE: At least it wouldn't be that one....

[HOSANNA grabs the perfume bottle and douses her arms and neck. CUIRETTE turns back to the window.]

HOSANNA: *[looking in the mirror]* Christ, are you stupid!

CUIRETTE: What?

HOSANNA: I was just telling myself how stupid I am....

CUIRETTE: You're just finding that out?

HOSANNA: Oh, no....

[*CUIRETTE looks outside, HOSANNA looks in the mirror.*]

CUIRETTE: You can't even see the end of the street....

HOSANNA: Cuirette, I'll never move ... and I'll never change my perfume.

CUIRETTE: You know, we'd be able to see all the way to Bélanger.... Look at the stupid thing. On, off, on, off, all night long. Every other sign in town goes off at midnight, but not this one. There are times I see red in my sleep.... On, off, on, off, on, off, on off.... He must be crazy, that guy, wasting all that money on electricity.... Hell, we're the only ones who ever look at his goddamn sign.

HOSANNA: That's right, we're the only ones....

CUIRETTE: And it's driving us nuts....

HOSANNA: It doesn't bother me.... It doesn't bother me in the least. In fact I'd even go so far as to say that ... I need it....

CUIRETTE: [*turning to HOSANNA*] Need it! What the hell for? What in the name of Christ could ...

HOSANNA: Cuirette, that sign ... Oh, never mind.... You'd only laugh, again....

[*Silence.*]

CUIRETTE: You know, it's funny, seeing you like that ...

HOSANNA: What?

CUIRETTE: ... with your make-up on and your dress off ... you look funny....

HOSANNA: But I'm not funny ... not the least bit funny. Not funny at all....

[*Long pause.*]

I'm ridiculous.

CUIRETTE: [*approaching her*] Come on, I don't think so....

HOSANNA: When I'm dressed like a man, I'm ridiculous. When I'm dressed like a woman, I'm ridiculous. But I'm really ridiculous when I'm stuck between the two, like I am right now, with my woman's face, my woman's underwear, and my own body....

CUIRETTE: [*putting his hands on her shoulders*] I don't think you're ridiculous....

HOSANNA: [*very softly, suddenly very tired*] Raymond, please, don't touch me....

CUIRETTE: Don't worry, I wasn't planning to.... The smell doesn't exactly turn me on....

[*HOSANNA throws her perfume bottle and breaks it.*]

HOSANNA: There, now it's really gonna stink! Go ahead, have your fit!

CUIRETTE: It's not me who wants to have a fit, Claude, it's you! But you're trying to keep it in, aren't you? You're trying to keep it in, but it's not going to work. And as for your fucking perfume, I've put up with it for four goddamn years, so it's not about to kill me now. Not even a gallon of it!

HOSANNA: Then why do you always talk about it!

CUIRETTE: Because, as you told me a few minutes ago, sweetheart, I got nothing else to say!

[HOSANNA coughs.]

There, you see, you're choking on it yourself. I told you it stinks in here. I better clean it up right now 'cause I know you won't do it, and if you cut yourself it'll be all my fault.

[HOSANNA gets up and goes to the window.]

That's right, see if you can see Bélanger.

[He bends down to pick up the broken glass.]

And if you're gonna be sick, do it in the bathroom. Christ, it stinks so bad in here we're gonna wake up the neighbours....

[He picks up her dress and hangs it in the closet.]

So ... into the closet with the Queen of the Nile, until her next appearance in society.... Hey, Hosanna, if you were to die all of a sudden, I think I'd have you embalmed in this thing!

[HOSANNA does not even react.]

I can see it now ... the look on people's faces ... especially your old lady ... Even for this I bet she'd have an explanation. "Don't be ridiculous, my dear, that's not a dress, it's ... just a fancy shirt. He was a very imaginative boy, you know, very creative." Man, I bet Sandra'd get a charge out of that, eh?

[Silence.]

I hung your dress in the middle of the closet. So every time you open the door it'll stare you right in the face, and you can suffer, baby, suffer....

[HOSANNA still does not react.]

I'm going to make the bed....

HOSANNA: Usually it's freezing on Halloween.

[CUIRETTE passes in front of the vanity mirror.]

CUIRETTE: That's what you should have busted....

HOSANNA: Not in a hundred years.... It's a souvenir ... like everything else.

CUIRETTE: How do you know what I'm talking about?

HOSANNA: *[very softly]* You just finished saying you were going to make the bed, Cuirette. As soon as you say that, I know everything you're going to do next.... Every night for four years you've done exactly the same thing. I don't even need to watch. That's how I know you just passed in front of the mirror....

[CUIRETTE moves the coffee table from in front of the sofa and starts to open the bed.]

And when you start to open up the bed, it's going to get stuck, and you're going to say "shit"....

CUIRETTE: Shit!

[HOSANNA shrugs her shoulders.]

HOSANNA: Then you're going to ask me, "When are we going to get rid of this thing?"

CUIRETTE: When are we going to get rid of this thing?

HOSANNA: And I'm going to answer ...

[She turns towards CUIRETTE.]

When you start working, Raymond, when you start working.

[She looks back out the window.]

Would you mind telling me what difference it would make if we could see down to Bélanger? There's probably another sign blocking the view anyway.

CUIRETTE: At least we wouldn't have that mother staring at us all the time. Oops, I almost knocked old David on his ass!

HOSANNA: Well, I think it's just fine, that sign ... just fine.... We should leave the window open tonight. Just think, it's November, that's really amazing. It's almost warm.

CUIRETTE: Yeah, and we'll be paying for it in January, you wait.... The bed's ready....

HOSANNA: No, not going to bed yet ... not tired....

CUIRETTE: You're working tomorrow.... It's Saturday, your heaviest day....

HOSANNA: No, not going in.... Besides, I won't sleep now....

[*CUIRETTE starts to get undressed.*]

You go to bed.... The sign'll go off any minute now.... It must be nearly four.... You'd think it would be chilly, eh.... I can't understand it....

[*Before he gets into bed,* CUIRETTE *looks at his erotic painting over the sofa.*]

CUIRETTE: I wonder if I could still sell my painting. That'd give me some bread for a while.

HOSANNA: Dreamer! Anyway, it's not yours to sell. You gave it to me. Besides, no one else would be sucker enough to hang that thing over their bed.

CUIRETTE: It's not half as bad as the crap they sell down at Place Ville-Marie. Maybe I oughta take it up again....

HOSANNA: I'd say it makes up for the sign and the perfume. Hey, Picasso, did you ever think of that? Your painting there, it doesn't smell, but Christ, it's ugly! It's as hard to stomach as my perfume.

CUIRETTE: I think about it a lot sometimes.... I don't know.... Maybe I will....

HOSANNA: *[still looking outside]* Look, make you a deal.... I'll take down the painting, and you can take down the sign....

CUIRETTE: It'd be nice to get back into that....

HOSANNA: Then we'll hang the sign in here and the painting outside.... The pharmacy will go bankrupt, and I'll get to keep the sign....

CUIRETTE: I don't know if I could still do it though.... I was pretty good in those days, you know, but for stuff like that, it takes a lot of ... concentration.

HOSANNA: In that case, you'd better forget it.

CUIRETTE: Oh, well, I'm going to bed....

[The phone rings.]

HOSANNA: If that's Sandra, tell her that besides being ugly, her dress was so short you could see her tampax sticking out....

CUIRETTE: She was wearing a long dress.... Hello....

HOSANNA: I know she was wearing a long dress, stupid!

CUIRETTE: Yeah....

HOSANNA: Tell her that her tampax was sticking out anyway. She had a long, long string on it.

CUIRETTE: Ah.... No.

HOSANNA: Is it her?

CUIRETTE: Yeah, but don't make it any earlier....

HOSANNA: Who is it?

CUIRETTE: Oh, no, we're not changing that....

HOSANNA: Cuirette, who is it? Is it Sandra?

CUIRETTE: Will you shut up! It's for me.

HOSANNA: Oh, la, la, I beg your pardon.... I understand, I understand. Excuse me, my lord.... I'll just withdraw into my apartments.... For once I'll tell myself to take a shit!

[She goes into the bathroom.]

CUIRETTE: Hi.... I didn't think you were gonna call. I was getting ready to go to bed....

[He laughs.]

Hell, no, I never do that by myself ... only when I'm desperate.

[Laughs again.]

Yeah, as a matter of fact, she phoned a while ago to invite me.... What do you think, is there gonna be any action?... Okay, great, I'll see you there. Oh, hey, you really missed something tonight.... Did you hear about it?

[HOSANNA comes out of the bathroom.]

Don't worry, she doesn't scare me....

[Seeing HOSANNA.]

Yeah, sure, we'll ... keep in touch.... See ya.

[*He hangs up.*]

HOSANNA: Did you ever see a woman pee standing up?... I was watching myself in the mirror ... Elizabeth Taylor, in profile, with this thing hanging out ... pissing.... Disgusting!

[*Pause.*]

HOSANNA: Who phoned? Some new snatch?

CUIRETTE: Why do you say it like that?

HOSANNA: Christ, you don't expect me to call them your girl friends, do you?

CUIRETTE: Yeah, it was some new snatch.

HOSANNA: For tonight?

CUIRETTE: Yep!

HOSANNA: Just like that, at four in the morning! I suppose that was arranged in advance, like everything else tonight!

[*Trying to be funny.*]

I think I'd better close the window, eh?... You never know what might happen ... a young girl, all alone in the house.... Ha, ha, ha. Aren't I funny? Oh, well, I suppose the best thing that could happen to me tonight just isn't going to happen....

[*She lets herself fall on the bed.*]

CUIRETTE: [*after a moment*] You want me to stay?

HOSANNA: No, I don't want you to stay.... I need you to stay, but I don't *want* you to.... Anything I might need doesn't matter anyway.... Go on, go out and get laid, it'll do us both some good. You and your big dick, me and my little pea-brain.

CUIRETTE: Who said anything about getting laid? I'm just going to a party at Sandra's....

HOSANNA: Jesus, are you naive! Sometimes I think you make a point of being stupid. You know perfectly well how Sandra's parties turn out. They're worse than a goddamn Fellini movie, for Chrissake! She must spend the next three days just getting the place picked up.... Picking herself up too, eh, or rather coming back down, after all the speed she takes.... And I'm warning you, eh, don't come home all speeded up like the last time. For three days you looked like a glass of Bromo Seltzer.

CUIRETTE: I felt like one too.... It was great....

HOSANNA: Yeah, sure, you were having a ball, but for me it was a pain in the ass.... It's all very well to feel like a Bromo, Cuirette, but when you've been fizzing for fourteen hours, I'd settle for indigestion!

CUIRETTE: What do you know about it, you farmer? You never tried anything.

HOSANNA: Cuirette, just watching you come down tells me a lot about your phony paradise....

CUIRETTE: Chicken shit....

[CUIRETTE starts getting dressed again.]

HOSANNA: Maybe so. But if you could see yourself after you've been shooting up, you'd be chicken too.

CUIRETTE: Who cares what you look like, it's what you feel that counts....

HOSANNA: Will you listen to her.... I can "feel" things without that, thank you.

CUIRETTE: You stupid twat! You never understand a thing!

HOSANNA: Tell me, were you taking drugs?...

CUIRETTE: Drugs!

HOSANNA: ... Back in your purple shit phase, were you taking drugs then? No! Are you still painting that purple shit today? No! What you were doing, Cuirette, was really ugly, but my God, at least it was something!

CUIRETTE: What I take has nothing to do with ... Man, you really know how to twist things, don't you?

HOSANNA: Listen, the day you found out your stuff wasn't worth shit, you didn't feel so good then, did you? You told me so yourself. You took acid, you looked at your paintings, and pouff, you couldn't create anymore.

CUIRETTE: Anyone can have bad trips....

HOSANNA: No, no, no, you don't take bad trips if you don't know how to handle them.

CUIRETTE: Which means *you* don't know how to handle them.

HOSANNA: That's right, and I'm not afraid to admit it.... What if I'd been stoned tonight?

CUIRETTE: Wow! I never thought of that. Would have been even funnier. Oh, yeah, I can just see it!

HOSANNA: On the other hand, that might have saved me.... It might have kept me from going up on that stage....

[Pause.]

So, you're off to Sandra's are you? Who is she, by the way ... your latest heart throb?

CUIRETTE: You don't know her....

HOSANNA: I know everyone who's gay in Montreal, my dear, even the ones who don't know it themselves. Unless, of course, she's fresh in from Drummondville, and I haven't had the pleasure of meeting her on the circuit ... yet. Can't you at least tell me her name?

CUIRETTE: Reynald.

HOSANNA: Reynald! She hasn't even taken a maiden name, and you're interested in him already! Is he nice and ladylike at least?

CUIRETTE: I don't know if he's "nice and ladylike," but he's a lot better looking than you!

HOSANNA: Well, my beauty, that's not so hard. Can't you do better than that?

> *[She goes over to her vanity table and sits down. She takes the pot of cold cream.]*

No.... No, I just can't do it.... That reminds me, lover boy, while you're out dancing a fugue with your new nymphette, see if you can arrange to stay away for a few days. My mother's arriving tomorrow, I forgot to tell you.... There's only room for two in this place, and since it's my bed and my apartment ...

CUIRETTE: You cocksucker!

HOSANNA: Watch your language, dear, you're getting vulgar. Since you've been putting on weight you have a tendency to get gross.

> *[Pause.]*

You should be happy.... Everything's working out fine.... You'd have had to go anyway.... Look, take Reynalda on a little honeymoon, why don't you? Then, when the fun's over ... if you feel like it ...

[Defeated, HOSANNA stops suddenly.

Very low.]

You're right, it stinks in here. And it's not the perfume either....

CUIRETTE: I don't believe you. It's not true your mother's coming tomorrow.

HOSANNA: Oh, yes it is, it certainly is....

CUIRETTE: You're just saying that to fuck me around....

HOSANNA: She phoned the day before yesterday ... or was it yesterday?... Anyway, she phoned....

CUIRETTE: You know I don't have a cent. You know I got no place to go.... I don't believe you....

HOSANNA: *[shouting]* Then don't believe me, goddamn it, but don't come back for three days, that's all!

CUIRETTE: I don't have to do whatever you say, you know....

HOSANNA: When it's me who's paying the rent, you do! Now listen, stud, you're going to that party? I'm telling you to go because I need my apartment. You can sleep wherever you like and with whomever you like, I don't give a shit, but I don't want my mother to walk in here and find you, is that clear, Einstein? I'm supposed to be living alone, see, so I don't want to get caught making out with some has-been motorcycle freak whose greatest disappointment in life was that he never got to be Marlon Brando's understudy!

CUIRETTE: What difference would it make? She's seen others, even though she pretended not to! Anyway, she's seen me....

HOSANNA: My mother doesn't know I'm the way I am, and ...

CUIRETTE: For Chrissake, Hosanna, you can smell your fuckin' perfume down on the street! All you gotta do is walk by, and you know there's a queer living in the place. You can find the right apartment by just following your nose! Besides, it's a waste of time hiding all your wigs, your gowns, your high-heels, your big sexy David there.... Your old lady never sees 'em anyway. The last time she popped in from Ste-Eustache, remember that, "Surprise, surprise?" I was here then, I saw how you two carried on. We'd just finished supper, eh? I was getting ready to do the dishes, and you were putting on your make-up, remember, 'cause you were going out that night. In fact you were putting on your make-up when she walked in the door, Hosanna. You didn't have time to turn your stinkbox here into a "straight" apartment, did you? The whole time she was here, she pretended to see nothing. Not a goddamn thing! After she kissed you she had to take a kleenex and wipe her mouth 'cause you had pancake all over your face. But she didn't say a word.... And all the time you were farting around in the closet looking for the "basic black number" you were supposed to wear that night, you know where it was? Draped over the only goddamn chair your mother could have sat down in! Still, not a word. Even when I shouted, "Has the mother-in-law arrived?" she didn't hear a thing. Nothing! I did it on purpose too, just to see what she'd do. When you introduced me to her, I had a frying pan in one hand, a dish towel in the other, and an apron around my waist. And I don't exactly look like a maid, do I, Hosanna! "How do you do," she says in her nice, polite voice, but she was looking three feet off to the side.... She only looked at me once.... I got up to take some things out to the kitchen, and when I came back I knew she'd been checking me out 'cause all of a sudden she looked away. And, right there, she gave you this sign of approval! Yeah, Hosanna, approval!... As if to say, "He's very nice, Claude. Your friend is very nice. I approve...." So if it's really true she's coming here tomorrow, and she finds me sleeping in your bed, she's gonna tell you the same thing, Claude, the same thing, "Your friend is very nice. I approve."

HOSANNA: You're wrong, Cuirette. She won't tell me the same thing.

CUIRETTE: You're fuckin' sick, the two of you.

HOSANNA: Besides, there's not much left to approve, so why disappoint her?

CUIRETTE: Well, at least you admit she knows....

HOSANNA: Okay, okay, she knows, she knows. So what!

CUIRETTE: So why do you two keep playing games? Why's she pretend she doesn't know?

HOSANNA: We talked about it once, Cuirette, and that was enough.

CUIRETTE: And I suppose you got it all straightened out, just like that....

HOSANNA: I'm the one who doesn't want to talk about it.

CUIRETTE: Huh?

HOSANNA: Look, you're all dressed, you're ready to go out, so go. Go, Raymond, go to your fucking party....

[HOSANNA gets up and goes towards the window.]

Me, I'll wave goodbye with my big white hanky.

CUIRETTE: One of the biggest queens in Montreal, and you can't even talk about it with your old lady.

HOSANNA: One of the biggest queens, are you blind? Not after tonight, I'm not. As for my old lady, sweetheart, I'm not afraid to talk to her about anything.... It's getting cold.... It's almost light ... and I'm standing here without a stitch.

[HOSANNA closes the window and goes to the closet. The first thing she sees, obviously, is the Cleopatra dress.]

Oh, you put it in a good place, that's for sure.

[She takes a dressing gown and puts it on.]

You want to know what she said when she found out I was gay? Huh? You want to know? I was in grade seven at Ste-Eustache, and they used to laugh at me because I looked so much like a girl.... Don't worry, Cuirette, this won't take long, I'm not a masochist. Besides, it makes no difference what they did to me, at least I got out. Which is more than I can say for the jerks in my class who were always feeling me up and writing "Lemieux's a queer" all over the johns. "Lemieux wants your hard on, so be hard on Lemieux".... No, I don't think about it much anymore, they were just a bunch of sick perverts anyway.... But her ... what she did to me, that's another story.

[Silence.]

She must have known long before I told her. Christ, everyone else knew. Which is to say, everyone had decided. They'd seen it, they'd figured it out, they talked about it, and they all thought it was very funny. When I realized the truth ... when I saw that to be queer doesn't just mean that you act like a girl, but can also mean you really want to be a girl, a real girl, and that you can manage to become one ... Christ, you can actually manage to become a real girl.... When I realized it was true, that the guys in my school, especially the older ones in the ninth grade ... attracted me ... I went straight to my mother. Jesus, how's that for being stupid! I was naive enough to think that ... she'd help me ... or at least explain it to me ... what it all meant.... My mother, who'd always kissed me and pampered me, and dressed me up, who never stopped telling me how dangerous women were and that I shouldn't go near them ... because she wanted to keep me all to herself ... to be her crutch in her old age, she said.... She was scared that some woman would come and steal me ... Bullshit!... You know what she said to me when I told her I'd begun to sleep with men? She said, "If that's the way you want to be, Claude, just make sure they're good-looking." That was it. Not another word. And she figured she could hold on to me.

[Silence.]

But the day I turned sixteen I was on my way to Montreal with the first trick I could lay my hands on. And then ... step by step ... little by little ... I became Hosanna ... Hosanna, the biker's girl friend! Hosanna, the stud's favourite hairdresser! Hosanna, the motorcycle queen! And ever since then, whenever she and I get together, we act like nothing's happened. She pretends she doesn't see a thing so she won't have to talk about it. As for me, I have no wish to entertain her with my "great erotic escapades." So there you are. That's it. The end of this touching and most unoriginal success story ... so touching and so second-rate....

CUIRETTE: How come you never told me that before?

HOSANNA: Raymond, there are times I hate that woman so much I don't know what to do to her, I don't know what. I was hoping I'd win tonight, because if I had, every paper in the city would have had my picture in it, and underneath my real name ... I would have insisted on my real name, Cuirette ... because that just might have killed her, the bitch!

CUIRETTE: How come you never told me....

HOSANNA: What difference would that have made?... I don't need anyone's pity....

CUIRETTE: You really are stupid. Why are you telling me now, for Chrissake! Just to keep me here longer?

HOSANNA: To keep you here ... Who do you think you are? You could have walked out anytime, Cuirette. Besides, I wasn't talking to you....

CUIRETTE: Fine, so go ahead and talk to yourself....

[He goes towards the door.]

HOSANNA: *[without looking at him]* By the way, you shouldn't wear your belt too tight.

CUIRETTE: What?

HOSANNA: Your belt, it's too tight, dear.... Your rolls are hanging out.

> *[CUIRETTE looks at his belly.]*

You'll never turn Reynalda on with all that sticking out over the top of your pants ... not unless she goes for fatsos....

> *[CUIRETTE comes back towards HOSANNA.]*

CUIRETTE: Look, I told you ...

HOSANNA: *[cutting him off]* I've been watching you get fat, Cuirette! You're fatter now than you were last week, and next week you'll be fatter still. If you go on eating like a pig and drinking beer like a fish, you'll split your pants and pop all your buttons.

CUIRETTE: That's not true!

> *[CUIRETTE adjusts his pants.]*

HOSANNA: You're not what you used to be, Raymond....

CUIRETTE: Alright, alright, I know, I'm not what I used to be.... I'm fat ... okay? I have a tough time getting into my pants, and I got no money to buy a new pair ... okay? I know all that, Hosanna, every bit of it. I was good-looking once, damn good-looking, and now I'm not anymore. And I also know why you're always reminding me of it. It's because maybe, just *maybe*, it helps you forget that you're getting old and ugly yourself. Yeah, that's right. When it comes to getting old, Hosanna, you're getting there fast.... But your problem isn't around your belly, sweetheart, it's in your face!

HOSANNA: If you don't shut your mouth ...

CUIRETTE: You just love to laugh at other people's faults. That's all you ever do is laugh at other people. But you got a taste of your own medicine tonight, eh? You finally found out what everyone thinks of you, eh? Well, maybe I'm fat, Hosanna, but at least I still grab 'em!

HOSANNA: He still grabs them! He still grabs them, alright! In the dark, yeah! In the meat racks, yeah! In the parks, in the back alleys, at the movies! In the toilets! Oh, it's true, Cuirette, you used to be good-looking once, but now, now, you're nothing but a washroom cowboy....

CUIRETTE: I don't have to go there, you know. I do it for kicks.

HOSANNA: Then where did you meet your Reynalda? Wasn't it at night? It couldn't have been during the daytime? I'll bet she doesn't have a clue what you really look like. Oh, how I'd love to be a little birdie so I could fly over to Sandra's and peek in the window, just to see Reynalda's face when she finally gets a good look at you.

CUIRETTE: I met Reynalda on the street in the middle of the day, Hosanna. And, by the way, it could be a lot more serious than you think....

HOSANNA: If you're trying to scare me, dear ...

CUIRETTE: I'm not trying to scare you, I'm just clueing you in. I might stay away longer than you think, you know....

HOSANNA: And what are you gonna do for money? You can't even buy gas....

[Pause.]

Eh?... You know I don't believe you, Cuirette. Okay, beat it. You've kept her waiting long enough. If you don't get your ass moving she's going to find someone else.... I'm giving you three days off. Then you can come back and cook my meals.... That's all you're good for anyway....

CUIRETTE: That's all I'm good for, eh? That's not what you say at night....

HOSANNA: What I say at night, my friend, or if you prefer, whatever noises I make while we're pretending to fuck, believe me, they're just my way of trying to convince myself I'm enjoying it. What we do together, Cuirette, for a long time, it's been nothing more than ... biology. I suppose you think your way of making love is pleasant for a ...

> *[HOSANNA stops suddenly.]*

CUIRETTE: For a woman.... Stopped yourself just in time, eh? You know, Hosanna, every time you play the queen, or whenever you're trying to be funny, and especially when you're trying to get your hooks into some new biker, since that's what you dig most, you're always a woman. And everybody's gotta know it. Even when we come back here, and I'm tired and you're horny—and don't give me that shit about not enjoying it, Hosanna, 'cause you love it so much you can't get enough—when you're horny and I'm not—yeah, when I'm the one who doesn't want it—you launch into the same routine, prancing around, wiggling your ass, soaking yourself in that piss you call perfume, just to get me all worked up.... But if we start fighting, or try to talk serious, you don't know what you are. You don't know if you're a man or a woman, Hosanna. You know it's stupid to call yourself a woman 'cause I can throw it back in your face like I'm doing right now. And you know it's even stupider to try to act like a man when you're dressed in those rags, and you got that shit smeared all over your face.... So what are you, Hosanna? Eh? Would you mind telling me just what the fuck you are?

HOSANNA: If I'm neither a man or a woman, then why do you stay with me? If you don't know what I am, who is it you go to bed with every night, the man or the woman? Answer me that, Cuirette, my pet. Is it my dresses that turn you on or is it me? Is it Hosanna, the drag queen, or Claude, the farmer? If Hosanna turns you on, then why do you sleep with a guy? And if it's Claude, then why do you sleep with a guy *who looks like a woman*? Eh? It couldn't be that you're scared of women, could it?

CUIRETTE: I'm not scared of women.

HOSANNA: Listen, toughy, have you ever touched a woman? Oh, you look tough alright, but for four years, guess what, you've been my maid. You realize that? We've been together four years, and for four years I'm the boss. I'm the one who goes out to work, I'm the one who feeds you, and you're the one who washes the floors, does the dishes, and cooks the spaghetti. Do you realize that? Oh, you're always bragging about how you live off me, but do you ever tell anyone who does the laundry, who picks up the broken glass? Out there, you cruise around town on your bike, but when you're home, you scrub the pans, and you take out the garbage. Me, I'm a hairdresser by day and a woman of the world by night.... But what are you? Huh? A cleaning lady who rides a motorcycle when she gets off work?

   [Pause.]

You never thought of that, did you, that between the two of us, you're the woman. And you know what I am? I'm the man of the house, Cuirette. I'm the man.

CUIRETTE: That's bullshit! You're not the man of the house. You might give the orders, but you give them like a woman.

HOSANNA: But I still give the orders....

CUIRETTE: If you were a man, you'd act like a man, at least when you're alone. But no, when you're alone, you go on behaving exactly like a woman. You never act like a man when you're anywhere near that goddamn mirror. And you sure as hell don't act like a man in bed.... Especially there!... Yeah! In four years you haven't done one single thing in bed that would make me think you were a man, not one! You live like a woman, and you fuck like a woman. And ever since the lines started showing around your eyes and in the corners of your mouth, your pancake's getting thicker, just like a woman. You've even started wearing it to work, for Chrissake. You can't go out of the house in daylight without putting half a pound of shit on your face. You're getting old, Hosanna. You're getting old the way a woman gets old ... fast! And it won't be long before you start getting all your crummy jokes about old queens right back in your face. It started tonight, and let me tell you, that's only the beginning. Just a few more wrinkles on your lovely puss, and then believe me, baby, the fur's gonna start flying. They'll be taking chunks out of you.... The same treatment you've been giving them all these years.

[Pause.]

It's all over, Hosanna. After tonight, you're through playing the spring chicken.

[He goes towards the door.]

You hear me, Hosanna? After tonight you're through.

[He opens the door.]

And you want to know something really stupid?

[Pause.]

I love you, goddamn it, I love you!

BANG

[He slams the door behind him. HOSANNA runs to the door and opens it, shouting.]

HOSANNA: Well, you know, sometimes I'd like to fuck you, Cuirette! Sometimes I'd really like to fuck you!

Who fucks who?

BANG

[*She slams the door. She goes towards the bed and lights a cigarette. CUIRETTE'S motorcycle can be heard driving away. HOSANNA runs to the window.*
Blackout.

The sign on the Pharmacy continues to blink.]

Act Two

[Half an hour later. HOSANNA, sitting up in bed, is smoking. She is still wearing her Cleopatra wig. The urn-lamp is lit. The pharmacy sign suddenly goes off. HOSANNA notices this right away and turns her head towards the window.]

HOSANNA: *[putting out her cigarette]* Well, that takes care of that. No sleep tonight, Cinderella.

[She puts the ashtray on the bedside table.]

And I'm out of cigarettes. Shit! Everything happens to me at once. Everything. Now, if Cuirette were here, he'd tell me in his big stupid voice, "Cleopatra didn't smoke, you know." For three weeks he's been driving me nuts with his Cleopatra.... Well, you can't blame him, can you?... For the past three weeks I've been driving him nuts with my goddamn costume.

"How do you know she didn't smoke? Listen, they were all drug fiends, those Egyptians, the whole goddamn bunch of them."

[Imitating CUIRETTE'S voice.]

"Like me, you mean?"

[Her natural voice again.]

"No, dear, not like you. They all made history."

[CUIRETTE'S voice.]

"Yeah, well, maybe you and me could make something else...."

[Natural voice.]

"Shut up, dummy, you're getting on my nerves."

[She gets out of bed.]

"Ladies and Gentlemen, you have just heard the fourteen thousand, two hundred and twelfth episode of our great love story, 'Cuirette and Cleopatra,' conceived, imagined, produced, and *lived* by Claude Lemieux and Raymond Bolduc." Raymond Bolduc! Christ, it should be against the law to call yourself Raymond Bolduc!

[She looks at herself in the big mirror.]

Some people, they have such ugly names, they don't deserve to live. That's why actors and transvestites change their names: because they-don't-deserve-to-live. Cha-cha-cha! A cigarette, a cigarette, my kingdom for a cigarette! Now, who in hell would give me a cigarette for this dump?

[Silence.]

My cheap little perfume factory, my two-bit whore house ... My God, it stinks in here. It's unbelievable how it stinks! But ... the show must go on ... and on ... and on ... and on....

[She goes to the vanity table.]

Mirror, mirror, on the wall, who is the fairest of them all? Shut up!

[She starts to laugh.]

Oh, well, La Duchesse ... she'll always be the funniest.

[Long silence.

HOSANNA *takes a jar of cream, then sets it back down again gently.*

The telephone rings. HOSANNA *turns and looks at it for a long while.]*

Good thing I wasn't asleep, eh?

[She gets up slowly and answers the phone.]

Hello, Genevieve Bujold!

[She listens for a while without saying anything.]

Sandra ... Sandra, listen.... Of course, I knew it was you, dear. Jeanne Moreau never calls me at this hour.... Listen, was it really all that funny tonight? Because if it wasn't, you know, I'd really appreciate it if you'd just bugger off.... Okay, please?

[Silence.]

Oh, it was that funny, was it?... Then by all means, dear, keep it up. Keep it up!

[She starts to hang up, then stops.]

Oh, Sandra, you don't happen to have a cigarette, do you?

[She starts to hang up again but stops again.]

Oh, by the way, Sandra, you got what you wanted. Cuirette left half an hour ago, and he'll be there any minute. So start playing with yourself, you fat pig. Start working up a nice big hard on!

[She hangs up.]

Jesus, that woman gets on my tits!

[She goes back to the vanity table, takes the chair, carries it downstage centre, and sets it down, back to the audience. She sits down, straddling the back of the chair.]

Two months ago, on one of those fabulous Friday nights when we were all lying around Sandra's club, and we were all plastered because we hadn't made any tricks ... one of those really fabulous Friday nights that might just as well have been a Thursday night, or a Tuesday night, or a Saturday night, but which this time happened to be a Friday night, Sandra plugged in the microphone.... Now, there was no show that night, so everything was unplugged, especially us girls, if you get my drift?... Anyway, Sandra plugged in the mike to announce her annual Halloween party, her annual costume bash that costs you an arm and a leg and only buys you a lot of shit.... Now, I couldn't figure out why she was using the mike because she'd just finished telling us all about her party, going around to all the tables.... So I figured she was just making it "official." Well, how stupid can you get! Then she told us with that big smile of hers ... the filthy bitch! I should have known something was wrong! I should have known!

[*Slowly.*]

She told us that this year the party was going to have a definite theme.... Now, she never mentioned anything about that before ... a definite theme that everyone would have to follow.... So up got La Duchesse, and between a few mouthfuls of scotch proposed we should all dress up like men and once and for all give ourselves a really good scare.... Me too, I thought that was funny as hell, but Cuirette ... Cuirette jumped up and shoved La Duchesse back into her chair ... and then ...

[*Silence.*]

Then Sandra told us that the theme we had to follow for our costumes was—are you ready for this—famous women of history! And I fell for it, Christ! I walked straight into the trap.

[*Silence.*]

But how could I have known they hated me so much? Me! My heart was in my mouth. I was all goose bumps. Jesus, my big chance. My big chance had finally come! Cuirette, the gazelle, comes leaping over to my table.... "Did you hear that, Hosanna, did you hear?" The bastard! Probably winking at Sandra like a goddamn flashlight. And me, so excited I didn't even notice! Then La Duchesse stood up and shouted, "Hey, Hosanna, don't forget to ask Elizabeth Taylor if you can borrow her diamond, eh?" Everybody laughed. Me too. I was so happy. God, I was happy! Babalu was already talking about coming as Scheherazade, Candy-Baby as Marilyn Monroe, and we all know who Brigitte was thinking of, don't we?... But there wasn't one person, not one, who dared mention Elizabeth Taylor.

[Silence.]

Because Elizabeth Taylor ... is mine! And they know it! Elizabeth Taylor's been mine for twenty years. The first movies I ever saw were Elizabeth Taylor movies. And the last movies I'm ever going to see will be Elizabeth Taylor movies. And someday, when I'm old-old-old and rich-rich-rich, I'm going to buy me a movie projector that will run nonstop, and I'll sit, and I'll watch Elizabeth Taylor make her entrance into Rome until I croak.

[Silence.]

I've drooled over Elizabeth Taylor, I've jerked off over Elizabeth Taylor! I've laughed like an idiot, I've bawled like a baby over Elizabeth Taylor, and I'll go on doing it over Elizabeth Taylor until I drop! I even skipped school to see Elizabeth Taylor make her entrance into Rome. And I'll sell my last false tooth, if I have to, to see her do that again!

[She laughs.

Long silence.

She shrugs her shoulders.]

Shit! What a pile of shit! Until now I was perfectly happy just to look at Elizabeth Taylor. I never let myself try to look like her ... at least not in front of other people ... not yet.... I wasn't ready yet! I wasn't deserving enough. Fuck me! Deserving enough! Me, Claude Lemieux, coiffeuse at la Plaza St. Hubert, I thought that someday I'd deserve to look like Elizabeth Taylor. And now ... Christ!

[Silence.

She closes her eyes.]

There were at least ... oh, at least two hundred thousand people, I think.... Oh, yes. At least two hundred thousand! Dressed all in different colours, on a set three miles long, with papier mache sphynxes, houses, temples, ruins, *doors,* yes, doors two hundred feet high, all made out of papier mache.... The crowd was roaring, dancing, screaming.... The papier mache doors opened, like gigantic church doors ... and thousands, millions of coloured birds that don't even shit went flying over the papier mache set.... Huge black slaves, their bodies glistening, lifted the chair onto their shoulders. The trumpets blared, the drums rolled, the sky ...

[Silence.]

The sky was wine-red and streaked with gold, Christ! And ... Hosanna made her entrance! Hosanna, borne aloft in her chair, her chair suspended on a double axle to keep her level, dressed like Elizabeth Taylor, in her hands a whip and a golden ball of papier mache; Hosanna was making her entrance into Rome! And all the while, the sign from the Pharmacie Beaubien was flashing its red and yellow lights in the mirror, and Cuirette was snoring....

[Silence.]

The sign from the Pharmacie Beaubien flashed its red and yellow lights in the mirror while Cuirette snored ... his arm around Hosanna as she made her triumphal entrance into Rome!

[HOSANNA opens her eyes, gets up, and looks again for a cigarette.]

Hey, doesn't anybody have a cigarette, for Chrissake?

[She sits down again.]

There were at least ... at least twenty-five thousand extras, I think ... all dressed in the most fabulous costumes! I've never seen such fabulous costumes!... And the set! God, it wasn't a set. It was a real city made out of real marble. They built a real city out of real marble with sphynxes and pyramids made of stones! The biggest, most beautiful set I ever saw. And the noise! Listen, they were screaming so loud, I thought my ears were going to burst. Then the procession began. Soldiers in chariots, real chariots, soldiers on foot, real soldiers too, you know why? Because they marched in perfect formation. Bands, marching bands, and all the girls, made up to their assholes, throwing real petals from real roses as if their lives depended on it, doing belly dances and you name it. Elephants ... yes, there were even real elephants! Then the marble doors, the real marble doors opened wide, and the crowd exploded....

[Silence.

HOSANNA trembles slightly.]

... And Elizabeth Taylor made her entrance! Borne aloft in her chair, her chair suspended on a double axle to keep her level, Elizabeth Taylor, the real Elizabeth Taylor—the one who started out in a dog show and who's going to end up to be the richest bitch in the world, with a diamond collar around her neck—the real Elizabeth Taylor, not the papier mache one, made her entrance into Rome, her arms folded across her real breasts, loaded with jewels, a serpent around her head, more beautiful ... Jesus, more beautiful than Elizabeth Taylor in *Cleopatra*....

[Silence.]

And I said to myself: one day, one day, you'll make your entrance too! Oh, it won't be much compared to that one, but it will be better than nothing.... And every drag queen in Montreal is going to shit blood!

[Silence.]

Well, my entrance ... into Rome ...

[Silence.]

WHO WAS IT THAT SHIT BLOOD, EH? WHO SHIT BLOOD!

[Silence.]

Three weeks, three whole weeks of my life wasted preparing for a flop! Three weeks of hysteria, three weeks of frazzled nerves, three weeks of charging all over the city getting this junk together, all the special creams and pancakes, the eyeliners, the fabrics, the jewellery, and all the other shit. Yes, shit! Three whole weeks to think up, design, "create" ...

[She jumps up, goes to the closet, and takes out the dress.]

... to "create" that! That! That worthless piece of shit! I designed it myself! I cut it out myself! I stitched and hemmed the motherfucker, and I put every pearl and sequin on it with my very own lily-white hands. And I wore the thing, in person! I've been dreaming of this goddamn dress for ten years.... And what's worst of all, what's worst of all, this is exactly the way I imagined it! Yesterday, I thought my dress was beautiful. Yesterday I thought it was even better than the one I'd been dreaming of.

[She throws the dress on the floor.]

Tragic flaw

If only I hadn't been so proud of the thing! If I hadn't been so pleased with my face! But Christ, I was pleased with everything. *Yesterday ... I was sure I was beautiful!* Yesterday ... Hosanna was finally ready to make her entrance into Rome.

[She calms herself a little.]

The taxi driver couldn't believe it.... My God, it's Elizabeth Taylor! You should have seen his eyes pop when I told him where I was going.... "Oh, come on off it, you mean you're not a real woman! I don't believe it, I don't believe it!" And every time he stopped for a red light, people pointed at the window, saying, "Look, it's Elizabeth Taylor, it's Elizabeth Taylor!" And then, when I got to the club ...

[Long silence.]

When I got to the club and started up the stairs ...

[She screams.]

Why is it always so perfect in my mind?

[She takes her dress in her arms and sits down again.]

Of course, I didn't sleep a wink all night. I kept telling myself, "Sleep, sleep, sleep, you've got to sleep, you'll have bags under your eyes." But ... I couldn't sleep.... I was dreaming! The drums were beating, and ...

[Silence.]

I watched Cuirette sleeping. He's beautiful when he's asleep. I didn't go to work. I told them I had a migraine. Shit, I hope Peter didn't singe my Jewish ladies.

[Silence.]

I started to get ready at eleven in the morning. No kidding. I took a bath, and I gave myself the works. Beauty balls, bath salts, olive oil, vinegar, beer, egg yolks, you name it. When I got out of there I looked like an angel food cake.

[She smiles.]

It was Cuirette who said that. I dried myself from head to toe, every corner. There wasn't a square inch of me that wasn't completely new! Cuirette wanted ... Cuirette wanted to rape me on the spot.... "You don't stink anymore," he kept telling me. "You don't stink!" Of course, I had some fun with him, eh?... I started parading up and down in the nude. "Baby, you gotta be dry, you gotta be dry, dry, dry, so the new new clothes you're going to wear, and the lovely paint job you're going to put on, don't pick up dirt or sweat. Baby, you gotta be clean! Virgin material! Untouched. Like Mary ... the mother of God!" I looked at myself in the mirror ... front view, profile, the back.... Oh, to be a swan!... I almost broke my neck doing that.... I'm still pretty ripe ... a bit small maybe, I mean statuesque, but the proportions are good. Bloody good!

[Silence.]

That afternoon about three o'clock, when I sat down to do my make-up ...

[She puts the dress down, takes the chair, and goes to the vanity table.]

I froze. Make that look like Elizabeth Taylor? My heart was beating so fast, I thought it was going to explode. But I said to myself, "Hosanna, it's now or never."

[She gently picks up a jar of base make-up.]

Slowly I picked up the first jar.... I was trembling a bit ... then ...

[She flings the jar to the floor.]

Even if I had been beautiful, it wouldn't have changed a thing. Being beautiful wasn't the problem. That had nothing to do with it. What they did to me had nothing to do with being beautiful. Okay, it's true. I got ahead in this town by being a bitch. So what.... I only did what everyone else does, it's just that I've got more talent for it than the others, that's all. I've got a big mouth, and I like to shit on people. I always have, and I always will. So what? The ones who get the shit, deserve the shit, every time!

[Pause.]

That's not true, Hosanna. You shit on people whether they deserve it or not.... Anything for a laugh.... Well, what the hell, if you don't look after yourself in this town, you'll end up in a dark corner, sitting on your meat like the rest of the wallflowers. Thanks, but no thanks! I didn't crawl out of Ste-Eustache with my tail between my legs to eat a dog's dinner in Montreal. My big mouth, that's all I ever had. Can I help it if it made me famous? Now I'm not saying I've got the biggest yap in Montreal, 'cause that's not true. I can think of lots of people who could outdo me anytime, like that fat pig Sandra, for instance. But it won't be long before ...

[She stops suddenly and comes back to sit downstage, bringing her chair with her.]

At first I just watched La Duchesse and Sandra at work. I studied every move they made. I saw how they'd watch everyone else, then shit on them, smack them on the ass, stick out their tongues at them, tear off their wigs and their false eyelashes, and ... I learned. I studied everything. I remembered everything. They thought I was some poor little Orphan Annie come to seek her fortune in the big city and that the big city would squash her like a little bird, but they were wrong. Jesus, they were wrong! Then, when I managed to lay my hands on ... My hands. That's one way of putting it.... When I managed to get my hooks into Cuirette, Sandra, who'd had her eye on him for a long time, finally deigned to notice me, the bitch, at which point I told her to go jerk off with a handful of thumbtacks. And that's when Sandra learned who I was! That's when Montreal learned to respect me! That's when I opened my big yap and started to talk back. There's nothing I wouldn't say, nothing I wouldn't do, to keep my hands on Cuirette and everyone else's off. Oh, maybe Sandra owned the joint, and maybe La Duchesse was the queen of the queens on the Main, but Hosanna was fixing her sights. Hosanna was preparing her entrance.

[She stops suddenly and starts trembling like a leaf.]

Still, I got to be friends with La Duchesse ... during one of her endless fights with Sandra ... and ... Shut up, Hosanna, shut up. Everything's finished.... Everything's fucked, the whole thing is fucked!

[A very long silence.]

It took me at least three hours to get enough shit on my face to look just a little bit like something that might vaguely resemble, from a distance, Elizabeth Taylor in *Cleopatra*.... Then the wig, which, by the way, took me two weeks to talk a client into loaning me, I put on the wig ... and I looked exactly the way I look right now ... minus what got washed away in the flood, of course. I put on the sequins, one by one, I put on the eyelashes, one by one.... It's the only way to do it, eh?... I redid my beauty spot ninety-three-and-a-half times, and I moved it twenty-six times because where Elizabeth Taylor's got hers doesn't look good on me ... but of course I wound up putting it in the same place as hers.... For once Cuirette didn't laugh.... He watched me very seriously.... Christ, if I'd known, if I'd even suspected, I'd have taken my nail file and shishkebabbed his two eyeballs. He must have been killing himself all day long trying to keep a straight face.... Anyway, by six o'clock I was ready for my dress, but the party wasn't till midnight. So I sat myself down, turned on the TV, and from six till eleven-thirty I didn't budge. For five-and-a-half hours I watched the CBC girls do their numbers, right to the bitter end of *Appelez-moi, Lise*. But then when they tried to stick me with a re-run of *La Symphonie Pastorale* with Michelle Morgan and Pierre Blanchard, I said, "Cuirette, that's it! Get me my dress, my big moment has come!" He helped me to get dressed. He even did up my hooks. He even had the nerve to tell me I didn't look too bad. And I took it as a compliment! Finally when everything was ... strapped into place.... I closed my eyes and stood in front of the mirror.... Then I opened them again. And that's when it hit me smack in the face. Cuirette was behind me.... I saw him smiling in the mirror ... and I knew.... I knew I shouldn't be going to that goddamn party. And suddenly I didn't want to go anymore! I didn't want to go, but ... I looked at myself ... *and I thought I was beautiful!*

JESUS CHRSIT! JESUS, JESUS, MOTHERFUCKING CHRIST!

[Silence.]

I told Cuirette to call me a taxi.... I asked him if he was coming with me or if he was going to take his bike.... He told me he'd rather take his bike and get there ahead of me so he could see me arrive. Christ, I was so blind, it's unbelievable, so fucking blind! As soon as he called the taxi, he was out the door.... Wait, that's not true.... He stood there for a minute.... He stood there staring at me with this funny look on his face ... and I thought he was going to say something nice! After that, he left.... The door slammed, the bike roared off, and that was that! The taxi arrived.... I went downstairs.... When I got in the car, the driver took one look at me and said, "Yeah, I know, you're going to Sandra's drag party." I was the fourth one he'd taken over there that night. People did not stop at every light and say, "Look, it's Elizabeth Taylor, it's Elizabeth Taylor!" But that didn't bother me.... It was dark in the car....

[Silence.]

All of a sudden, I got scared again. My teeth were shaking, my knees were shaking, my balls were shaking.... *And before I knew it, we'd arrived at Sandra's club.*

[The door opens slowly, and CUIRETTE walks in.]

CUIRETTE: *[after a long silence]* I didn't go to Sandra's party....

HOSANNA: *[after a silence]* Cuirette was waiting for me at the door with ...

CUIRETTE: *[a little louder]* I didn't go to the party....

HOSANNA: ... with La Duchesse ... dressed as a man!

CUIRETTE: I went for a ride instead ...

HOSANNA: I should have stayed in the car! I should have stayed there and locked the door when I saw La Duchesse dressed as a man on Halloween. Right there, I should have understood everything.

CUIRETTE: ... in Parc Lafontaine. I went back to Parc Lafontaine.

HOSANNA: The first thing I saw when we turned the corner was Cuirette with La Duchesse.

CUIRETTE: Nobody there.

HOSANNA: Dressed as a man.

[*Silence.*

Nothing moves.]

CUIRETTE: I checked every path, made as much noise as I could, yelled my head off.

HOSANNA: When I got out of the taxi, La Duchesse came charging over, but Cuirette wouldn't let her speak to me. She started yelling, but she was so drunk I couldn't tell what she was saying....

CUIRETTE: They've fucked me, Hosanna! They've really fucked me up!

HOSANNA: If La Duchesse had been able to warn me, none of this would have happened!

CUIRETTE: I don't like it when things get changed. "You bastards, you've gone and changed it all around, eh, you've changed it around! You pigs! You're scared there'll be a few dark corners left, eh, so you put your fuckin' lights up all over the place! Well, tough shit! From now on we'll do it right under your noses!" I'm telling you, Hosanna, if I'd seen a cop I woulda run him down. "From now on we're gonna do it in public, goddamn it! And if there's lots of fags who ride bikes, there's just as many fags in the fuckin' police force, and that's a fact! So why don't we do it together, eh! We'll all get under the lights, drop our pants, and go to it right in the middle of the fuckin' baseball field!"

[Silence.]

If I'd seen a cop ... I probably would have run like hell, as usual....

[Silence.]

The bastards have changed everything, Hosanna! Even Parc Lafontaine....

[Silence.]

This is the only place I know where nothing changes. The only place where time just stops.... You know?... I don't want things to change!

[Very softly.]

You know what I mean?

HOSANNA: I tell you, the receiving line was a bit sparse. No fan-fares, no extras.... When I started up the stairs my balloon was already half-popped.

CUIRETTE: I didn't think it'd go that far....

HOSANNA: The further I got up the stairs, the more I could feel something was wrong.... Then all of a sudden I heard La Duchesse scream, "Don't go in, Hosanna, don't go in!"

CUIRETTE: It wasn't my fault....

HOSANNA: I didn't even have to open the door.... It opened by itself.... It was a little darker than usual, I couldn't see what was going on.... I went in.... I went in, goddamn it, I went in!

CUIRETTE: I almost told you before I left, but ... everything was ready ... and ... I thought ... Shit, I didn't think they'd go that far....

HOSANNA: Then the lights went on, every light in the place.... For a second I thought they had a nice surprise for me.... Oh, they had a surprise, alright.... But it wasn't quite what I had in mind....

CUIRETTE: They didn't tell me they were going to go that far, Hosanna.

HOSANNA: Everybody ... was dressed ... like Elizabeth Taylor in *Cleopatra*.

[Long silence.]

CUIRETTE: Sandra just said that ...

[Very long silence.]

It's awful, Hosanna, they've stuck their lights all over the place!

HOSANNA: The whole gang! Every single one! Babalu, Candy, Mimi, Lolita, Brigitte, Carole, and ... Sandra! Every bitch in the place! And every one of them dressed up better than me! Every one made up better than me!

[Pause.]

I looked like a beggar!

[Pause.]

They all acted as if nothing was wrong.... Me, too.... I acted as if nothing was wrong. Christ, I felt my whole body was exploding, I felt like I was falling into a pit, I could hardly breathe, for

Chrissake! But I didn't flinch. I just stood there staring into the room.

[Throughout the following two speeches, both characters speak at once, in the same tone, at the same speed. It is not important that one be heard more than another. CUIRETTE speaks to HOSANNA, but HOSANNA does not listen and talks to herself.]

CUIRETTE: They just said they wanted to play a joke on you ... 'cause you've gotten to be such a pain in the ass.... And you've been giving me a pain in the ass, too, Hosanna. I'm sick to death of your stupid games, and your smart-ass remarks, and your god-damn scenes that never end.... I thought they just wanted to ... teach you a lesson.... I let Sandra drag me into it.... You know what she's like.... And ... well, it was fun getting everything ready with her, Hosanna.... We'd worked it all out, every detail. There was no way it wasn't going to work.... And it did work.... And I laughed when I saw you arrive with your nose in the air, so sure of yourself in your cheap little outfit.... And I laughed when you went in there, and they turned on the lights.... I laughed at everything, Hosanna, I laughed at everything.... Because I hated you! If you only knew how much I've hated you these last few months! But now ... I see what they've done to you, Hosanna....

HOSANNA: I could have strangled them all with my bare hands! I could have skinned them alive, the bitches! But I said to myself, "Hang on, Hosanna, get a hold of yourself. You've got to act like nothing's happened. If you do anything you'll only make it worse." I was standing in the door, and no one was looking at me. But I could feel everyone watching me out of the corner of their eyes to see what I was going to do. Everyone was waiting for me to turn away so they could look at me. They were all waiting for me to crack, to collapse on the floor yelling and screaming. But I didn't.... I just stood there. And I wasn't looking at anyone either. I was looking at the mirror ball that had just started turning, pouring splotches of red and yellow light on my face. Red and yellow lights!

[Silence.]

Hosanna had made her entrance into Rome, and everyone was dressed like her! Only better!

[Silence.]

CUIRETTE: I don't know how to tell you this....

HOSANNA: Slowly I walked into the room full of Cleopatras. I sat down at my usual table. The waiter, who was all decked out in some kind of white toga, came over with a drink.... He said it was the evening special, "The Cleopatra Special!" Brigitte burst out laughing at the next table to me. Carole poked her one to shut her up. I drank my "Cleopatra Special." It was ginger ale.

[Pause.]

And then Cuirette ... Cuirette came over and sat down in front of me with a big smile on his face.

[HOSANNA looks at CUIRETTE for the first time since he came in.]

Cuirette, have you got a cigarette? I'm dying!

[CUIRETTE takes out a pack of cigarettes, takes one out, gives it to HOSANNA, and lights it. Then he goes behind HOSANNA and puts his hands on her shoulders. He will stay like that until the end of HOSANNA's monologue.]

Sandra, who by the way, makes a very fat Cleopatra, climbed up on the stage to get her show rolling. The same stupid jokes: "Good evening, Ladies and Gentlemen, and others...." The same boring crap she's been dishing up for years ... followed by the same boring songs she's been trying to sing for years.... People laughed, as usual, in the same spots, as usual.... But I was looking at you, Cuirette. And you were doing everything you could to avoid looking at me. Oh, you were having a ball. You could hardly wait. You could hardly wait for the fat pig to call out my name so I'd have to go up on that stage and show off my rags!

[Pause.]

When she announced that the contest was going to start, I nearly had a hemorrhage. I wanted to throw my second ginger ale right in your face, just to make you look at me ... and then to get out, out, out! But no! I had to stay. I had to prove ... that I'm strong, that I don't care about all your stupid jokes. I had to show them that Hosanna can take anything and that she's not just anybody! If you only knew, Raymond!

[Pause.]

They started with Bambi. Of course, all her friends thought she was fabulous. I watched her. She was beautiful. Next, it was Candy's turn. Now, Candy's a real dog, eh, but for once ... she almost made it. They were cheering and whistling.... The third Cleopatra was Carole. With a full-length dress it was almost bearable, considering her legs don't grow in the same direction. After that ... my turn. I don't know if you've ever heard a silence like that, Cuirette.... I know I haven't. When Sandra called, or rather screamed, my name, you'd have thought someone had cut off the sound. For a second I sat there nailed to my chair.... I think I was already dead. Then I don't know who, but someone began to shout, "Hosanna, Hosanna, Hosanna, Ho!" Then they all started banging their tables, yelling, "Hosanna, Hosanna. Come on, Liz, strut your stuff!" You were laughing so hard, Cuirette. You were laughing so hard, it was you that made me decide to go up on that stage! So I got up ... and I climbed the three steps, everyone shouting, "Hosanna, Hosanna," all around me.... And right there, in the middle of the stage, with everyone laughing at me and whistling and calling me stupid names, I said to myself, "Cleopatra is a pile of shit! Elizabeth Taylor is a pile of shit! You asked for your pile of shit, Hosanna-de-Ste-Eustache. Well, here it is. Your big pile of shit!" Now listen, Cuirette, I wasn't Cleopatra anymore. I was Sampson, do you hear me? Sampson! And right there, I completely destroyed my papier mache set! Because you had completely destroyed my papier mache life.

[*Pause.*]

I never knew you all hated me so much....

[*HOSANNA puts her head against CUIRETTE'S stomach.*]

I'm a man, Raymond. If I ran out of there like that, tumbling down the stairs, almost breaking my bloody neck, if I ran out, Raymond, it's because ... I'm not a woman.... And you're going to have to get used to that....

[*Silence.*

Complete change of tone.]

Why didn't you go to the party?

CUIRETTE: I didn't feel like it.... Anyway, you're the one who sent me....

HOSANNA: And Reynalda?

CUIRETTE: Reynalda can find someone else.

HOSANNA: So she really does exist?

CUIRETTE: Of course she does.

HOSANNA: Ohh, it's not like you to let go of an easy catch....

CUIRETTE: I'll find her again.... You're not in bed yet?

HOSANNA: I was a while ago, but I couldn't sleep....

CUIRETTE: No wonder, with all that crap on your face....

HOSANNA: I didn't feel like taking it off.

CUIRETTE: It's hot in here....

HOSANNA: Open the window....

CUIRETTE: We'll freeze....

HOSANNA: Then don't complain....

> [*HOSANNA gets into bed. CUIRETTE starts getting undressed.*]

The stink doesn't bother you?

CUIRETTE: [*slight pause*] What stink?

HOSANNA: I guess I can sleep now....

CUIRETTE: Now that I'm back....

HOSANNA: [*slight pause*] Yes, now that you're back.

CUIRETTE: Hosanna....

HOSANNA: What....

CUIRETTE: What about your mother?

HOSANNA: What about her?

CUIRETTE: Is she really coming?

HOSANNA: Of course she is.

CUIRETTE: What are we gonna do?

HOSANNA: She can sleep on the floor.... Come on....

CUIRETTE: Hosanna ...

HOSANNA: What!

CUIRETTE: I guess there's no point in saying I'm sorry....

HOSANNA: You're right....

[CUIRETTE *gets into bed.*]

CUIRETTE: You know ... Ah, I can't seem to tell you anything without wanting to shout.... When I was cruising around on the bike a while ago, I was thinking about what you told me.... The important thing is ... Jeez, I feel stupid telling you this.... The important thing is that you be yourself, that's all. I think that's all.... Claude ... it's not Hosanna that I love....

[*Silence.*]

Take off your make-up.... Go on, take it off....

[HOSANNA *gets up and sits down at her make-up table. She removes her wig and takes off her make-up. She looks at herself in the mirror.*

HOSANNA: Cleopatra is dead, and the Parc Lafontaine is all lit up!

[*She gets up, takes off her underpants, and turns slowly towards* CUIRETTE.]

Look, Raymond, I'm a man.... I'm a man, Raymond.... I'm a man. I'm a man.... I'm a man.

[RAYMOND *gets up, goes towards* CLAUDE, *and takes him in his arms.*

Slow Fade.]

Does he want Ray to say "No, you're Not"

What are imposed roles, necessary roles, Chosen roles for these two "men"?

Printed in Canada